HOW TO SELL
YOUR HOUSE
FOR MORE THAN
IT'S WORTH

HOW TO SELL YOUR HOUSE FOR MORE THAN IT'S WORTH

Jerry Pennington and Fred G. Schultz

Ꝙ⅋P

A Playboy Press Book

Library of Congress Cataloging in Publication Data

Pennington, Jerry.
    How to sell your house for more than it's worth.

    1. House selling. I. Schultz, Fred G., joint author.
II. Title.
HD1379.P37   658.89'643   76-17637
   ISBN 0-87223-467-3

Contents

Preface

For most Americans the sale and purchase of a house is their largest personal business venture. Unfortunately, all too many of us are totally unprepared for this transaction. Frequently one leaves the sale of their home with this gnawing feeling that they sold too cheap. In fact, this is many times true. All too often two identical homes on a block will sell for vastly different prices. The reason is often good marketing skills rather than good real estate skills.

This book is not meant to be a course in real estate, nor is it designed to teach you about the various aspects of home selling. It is specifically designed as a pragmatic guide to getting the best possible price for your home. The techniques are all proven in the marketplace.

The book calls for no prior real estate experience or any special skills. Rather it is a detailed systematic guidebook to properly handling the sale of your home. I know you'll find the techniques interesting. But, most important of all they will put money in your pocket. An evening spent studying (not just reading) this book will return big dividends.

Jerry Pennington

HOW TO SELL
YOUR HOUSE
FOR MORE THAN
IT'S WORTH

CHAPTER
1

How to Get Your House Ready for Sale

Most homeowners consider remodeling an investment. When it comes time to sell their house, they usually expect to at least recover their costs, perhaps even turn a profit. Well, let's explode that myth right now. First of all, rarely half of what is spent redecorating or remodeling is ever recovered. And in some cases, an "improvement," like a pool, can make your house *harder* to sell—especially to families with very young children. When you consider remodeling your house to make it more salable, you have to evaluate the purpose of every dollar spent—in relation to the return you'll get in the sale of your home.

What appears to be essential remodeling to you may end up being an unnecessary frill to a prospective buyer. Remember, you've lived in your house for a while and its deficiencies have softened, if you haven't forgotten them altogether.

Don't make the mistake of renovating to correct an inconvenience you have suffered, until you determine whether you'll get that money back when you sell. For example, if you had frequent overnight guests but no separate guest room, you probably became burdened with the problem of extra sleeping arrangements. Spending money to convert your basement into a guest room might seem to be a worthwhile expense. When you sell you probably won't recover any of these costs. A finished basement is not an essential ingredient for a successful sale. It might add to the list of "extras" you use in your sales pitch, but it will not increase the value of your house. Here's another myth explosion: A $10,000 pool does not usually add more than two or three thousand dollars to the price of a house.

The risk of extravagant remodeling is that a homeowner can price his or her home out of the neighborhood range. If the price of homes in your neighborhood is around $35,000, spending $15,000 on a new kitchen and bathrooms could make your house worth $50,000, but unsalable at that price.

The advice in this book is based on the assumption that you have a limited amount of money to get your house ready for sale. Spend your money on those things that: 1. Will be of obvious appeal to prospective buyers. 2. Will let you recover your costs, if not increase the price of your house. 3. Will help you make a quicker sale.

As you read this section, put yourself in the role of a prospective buyer. Take an unbiased look at the condition of your house. What would the buyer see as he approached your front door? What would he or she think were the major drawbacks?

The Exterior

The outside of your house is the top priority. The gutters and paint job are what the buyer sees first and will create an immediate attitude toward the rest of the house. No matter how lovely the inside, flaking paint, an unkempt lawn or a littered driveway will be serious strikes against you.

The first thing to do is go outside and take a close look at your house. Stand in the street in front of your house. This is where your buyer will begin an inspection. Look at your lawn. Are there brown patches where there should be grass? Have weeds taken over? What about those bushes near the front door? Are they dying or in need of a good trim?

If you have three weeks or more before you put your house on the market you could spend as little as $15 on a bag of fertilizer, seed and weed killer. In one afternoon you could rake up any debris, turn the earth and reseed. Three weeks later you will notice a marked improvement in the appearance of your grass. The buyer will notice it too.

A local supermarket is a good enough place to buy inexpensive, sturdy bushes and ground cover. For as little as $10 or $12 you could improve the entrance to your house by planting an attractive grouping of bushes. A few ground-cover plants could hide the brown area around the tree on your front lawn where grass has always refused to grow. Don't forget to prune unsightly dead branches on bushes and trees and trim weeds and grass around walks and driveways. Most of the work involved in improving the appearance of your landscaping depends on how much time and energy you have. An outlay of $25 to $30 is really all you may need for materials, assuming you already have some foundation plantings and attractive groupings.

Hiring a professional gardener to do this kind of work can cost $100 or more. If you can't do the work yourself, hire local high school students to do it for you. For a flat rate of $2 or $3 an hour they could get your lawn in shape in a day or two. The only other costs involved would be for fertilizer, seed, weed killer and two or three bushes or shrubs.

There are certain jobs that should not be handled by an amateur. If your driveway needs resurfacing, a messy job could end up costing more to repair than if a professional had been called in the first place. If cracks or small potholes are all that need repair, the average homeowner should be able to complete the job for less than $50. Otherwise, be prepared to spend up to several hundred dollars for professional asphalt work. A less expensive alternative is to resurface your driveway with pebbles or rock chips. A 2- or 3-cubic-yard load of rock can be dumped for as little as $90. But be prepared to spend the good part of one day shoveling and then raking the rock chip onto your driveway. It's back-breaking work but it could save you $500 or more over the cost of asphalt resurfacing. Rock chip and pebbles promote good drainage. If you have a water problem in your driveway, pebbles are not only attractive but practical.

If there is no path or walkway to your front door, rock chip is an attractive, cheaper alternative to flagstone or brick. You do not need a professional mason (which could cost a few hundred dollars) and pebbles or rock chip should cost less than one-third as much as brick or flagstone. Dig an area three feet wide by three or four inches deep, the length of the path you want. Shovel your rock in. Level with a garden rake. The convenience and beauty of a path are a cosmetic addition to your house. Your walkway should run from the sidewalk to the front door, from the garage to the house and around to other entrances.

Inspect any fencing on your property. Now is the time to repair and replace loose boards in picket fences, replace worn-out hinges on gates and repaint rusty wrought iron railings. All these improvements can be made fairly quickly, and more than pay for themselves.

After you've completed the inspection and repair of your lawn, foundation plantings, drives, walkways and fencing, turn to the house itself. Go out into the street again and *objectively* consider the condition of the paint on the outside of the house. Those worn spots near the front door and chipped paint near the garage may have been overlooked by you in the past but a prospective buyer *will* notice them. If a buyer feels that a complete repainting of your house is necessary he will certainly deduct that cost (upwards of $1,000) from the price he is willing to pay.

There are certain shortcuts you can take to avoid the cost of repainting your entire house. If you can't get away with touching up the bad spots with the same color paint, an alternative is to paint just the front of your house. This is the side buyers will see first. And it will serve almost as well, that is, to give a good first impression. If it is essential to repaint the exterior on all sides, do it yourself if possible (but don't endanger yourself). High school students could do the job in a few days and save you hundreds of dollars. You won't get a masterful job, but the house will look many times fresher and more appealing.

Remember when choosing new colors, if you repaint completely, that the beautiful mauve you've always had a passion for will not appeal to all buyers. You'd be better off to stick to white or a pastel color to avoid shocking your prospective buyer.

Painting is the single best way to improve the exterior of your house. It can hide unsightly features or on the other hand even emphasize special details and lines. It can either add weight or soften the hard edges of poorly placed details. Painting any new additions the same color as the house adds to the whole exterior line. You can make a small house look larger by painting it white or using just one color. An awkward window can all but disappear if painted the same color as the rest of the house.

A combination of different window styles can take away from the attractiveness of the front of the house. By painting all windows, trim and walls the same color you can eliminate their obtrusiveness. Paint the entrance door a different color. It will draw attention to itself and away from any faults in the architecture.

One word of caution when buying exterior house paint. The best paints are expensive, but bargain paint may end up costing more when you have to paint three coats to cover an area where one coat of better paint would have done the job. Make sure you buy paint that is compatible with the existing paint or the new coat of paint will separate after it dries. Weather conditions also affect the appearance of a paint job. Painting when it is either below 50 degrees or above 95 degrees will cause the paint to dry improperly and could necessitate a complete repainting.

If your exterior walls show stains there are a few alternatives you might try before you consider a complete repainting. Those stains on parts of your house that are sheltered from rain may disappear with a stiff long handled brush and some detergent. If the results are not satisfactory, try a solution of one pound of trisodium phosphate in a gallon of hot water. Rubber gloves should be worn to protect your hands. A final thorough rinsing with clear water should eliminate most stains.

If metal staining near gutters or screens are a problem, bleaching them out with a solution of ¾ of a pound of oxalic-acid crystals in a gallon of hot water applied with a sponge might help. You may have to repeat the procedure two or three times to lighten it sufficiently to be unobtrusive. (It is all but impossible to remove metal stains entirely.) Remember when handling any of these chemicals to take all precautions listed on the package before beginning your work.

If gutters and metal trim are in disrepair you must first sand off all old paint before you apply a fresh coat. Chemical rust removers are also available and should be applied before you begin to paint. The new rust-proof paint is a good idea when repainting gutters, wrought iron or metal trim.

One of the most important areas of exterior work is your roof. Between $500 to $1,000 is the average price for a new roof, depending on the size of your home. If your roof is in complete disrepair the cost will most likely be deducted by the buyer from the price of the house. It is, therefore, important to spend some time and energy correcting any deficiencies that might exist.

There are a number of items that should be looked into when checking your roof. Begin your inspection on the underside of the roof; be sure to examine overhangs. Look for discolorations that would indicate leaks to a buyer or to a buyer's inspector. Check shingling to see if one or more missing shingles could be causing the leak. Replacing shingles is a relatively easy and inexpensive job, and does not require the services of a professional. All it takes is a good ladder and sturdy footing. A damaged or missing shingle should be replaced with a new shingle of the same composition. In the case of wooden shingles, repair by cutting and inserting under them roofing paper that is slightly larger than the shingle being replaced.

An afternoon's work is all that it will take to clean up and take care of the odds and ends around the outside of your house. Children's toys should be removed from the front lawn and steps. Garbage cans would look much better stored on the side or in the back rather than on the sidewalk in front of your house. Make sure ice has been salted or removed from your front walk in winter, and that wet slippery leaves have been swept away in the fall. Take some time to oil sticking hinges on your front door, and be sure the front doorbell is working. A broken ground floor window is not only unsightly, but may give the buyer the idea that your house has been forcibly entered even in a seemingly safe neighborhood.

A few hours with some brass polish and spray lacquer can dress up the exterior brass work around doors, lampposts and mailboxes. Make sure these are in top condition because they are surprisingly noticeable features and should be shown to their best advantage.

Now, let's survey the interior of your house.

The Kitchen

The kitchen is far and away the most important room. An unattractive kitchen can kill a potential sale, even before the buyer decides to inspect the rest of the house. Whatever you decide to invest in kitchen improvements is money well spent. It is the one room where you can almost always expect to recover at least 100 percent of your investment.

Spending some time and money on improving your kitchen can only increase the chances of a fast and profitable sale. As a general rule of thumb, you can spend up to 10 percent of the value of your house on a kitchen renovation and expect to add that percentage to the price of your house. (If you have a house in the $35,000 range, an outlay of $3500 would be high but reasonable.)

There are many improvements that can be made for as little as $25 to $200 that can achieve almost the same effect as a major renovation and give you profits to boot!

The three most important qualities of a good kitchen are proper appliance placement, adequate storage space and adequate counter space. If your kitchen suffers glaring drawbacks in any one of these categories it will pay you to make some improvements. It is not essential that you call in a kitchen planner or architect, because there are a number of improvements you can make on your own with little or no expense.

Proper appliance location means only that there should be as few steps as possible between major kitchen appliances. You should not have to walk the length of the kitchen to get from the sink to the stove.

It might cost $100 or more to move your kitchen sink from one place to another because plumbing pipes will have to be re-routed, or possibly be replaced if they are old and worn. Think twice before you relocate your sink. See if other appliances or furniture can be moved first.

Now take a good look at your kitchen appliances, especially the ones that you will be selling with the house. Is the enamel on your refrigerator badly scratched? The chrome handles rusted? If it is not frost-free, has the ice been removed from the freezer compartment?

With a small can of appliance touch-up paint the enamel on your refrigerator can look almost new. Repainting the entire refrigerator is another possibility, maybe harvest gold or another of the new colors that can go a long way toward brightening up a kitchen. A little chrome paint can do wonders for rusted handles. If your refrigerator is really old and you're thinking of purchasing a new one, put the old refrigerator in the basement or garage. If your refrigerator is old but adequate, spend $5 or so on some appliance paint and see if you can't make it more presentable.

If your stove is in good condition (or just needs some stiff cleaning) do not invest your money on a fancy self-cleaning stove. Whether your stove cleans itself or not will not materially affect the sale. A buyer would much rather put up with a less than luxurious stove if the rest of your appliances are up to par.

Now take a closer look at the kitchen sink. What kind of condition is it in? Is the porcelain chipped or scratched? Are the faucets operating satisfactorily?

The sink itself is the least expensive appliance in your kitchen. Surprisingly, a new faucet could cost almost as much as an entire sink and sometimes more. If your faucet is working and in good shape, replacing your sink would cost as little as $30. Before considering a new sink, consider an investment of $1.95 for some special porcelain paint that could change the appearance sufficiently. Again, an inadequate sink will not lose you a house sale, but it does help to set the tone for the appearance of your kitchen.

A fifty-year-old sink on legs is not the height of attractiveness. But building an inexpensive wooden cabinet around the base could make even an old sink presentable. If you are not especially handy with carpentry, a professional would charge somewhere in the neighborhood of $40 to $50 to do the job for you.

Dishwashers used to be considered a luxury. But more and more new homeowners expect them to be part of the kitchen plan. If you do not own a dishwasher and your house is large enough for a family, consider investing $125 in a convertible model—one that is used as a portable now but can be built-in at a later date. It is not necessary to buy a model endowed with features that are never used; a wash-rinse-and-dry cycle model is usually more than sufficient for an average family.

Adequate counter space is the next major consideration you might have to remedy. There are a number of solutions to this problem without spending hundreds of dollars. One idea for the small kitchen is to install pull-out cutting boards and counter-tops that slide underneath the existing counter. The most advantageous spot for these extensions would be in the space above the drawers closest to your range. This is where extra space is usually needed for cutting or mixing. A slab of maple approximately ¾" x 16" square should be adequate for the average cook.

Another solution to consider: a horizontal extension with cabinet space added under it. Of course, it must be positioned where it won't interfere with movement in the kitchen. If you have a larger kitchen with open floor space in the middle, an island counter-top is an ideal way to gain attractive extra work space, and could even incorporate either a new sink, stove or extra cabinets and drawers.

If you already have good counter space but its appearance leaves something to be desired, there are less expensive ways to improve appearance short of complete replacement. If there are badly worn spots, insert cutting boards in those areas that show greatest wear. Re-covering an existing counter-top with linoleum is far less expensive than Formica and can be installed without a carpenter. One of the most attractive ways to cover up flaws is to remove the existing counter entirely. (It should lift right off the supporting cabinets.) Install ceramic tiles (laid over a sheet of ¼-inch plywood that has been cut to fit). Tile costs vary with the type you choose, from fifty cents each for the kind usually found on bathroom walls to $5 each for hand-painted imported tiles. (A medium priced good-looking tile, covering an area of about 24" x 22" would run about $25.) After the tile is pasted to the plywood with a mastic solution, build a frame around the front, back and sides with pre-cut molding, then grout between the tiles. If the counter is in an area where food is prepared, a grout sealer is a good idea to eliminate stains.

Unless you can spend a few hundred dollars on new cabinets, concentrate on improving the efficiency of the space you already have. A broom closet, for instance, can become a small pantry with the addition of shelving. Mops and other cleaning equipment can then be stored in a hall closet or with specially designed hooks on the backs of doors. Circular, lazy-Susan shelves can be purchased at a local lumberyard and installed in corner cabinets—increasing storage capacity 100 percent or more.

Another alternative for you to consider is open shelving, usually no more than one-can deep, hung on open wall space behind a door or on swinging tracks, allowing a regular kitchen cabinet to become a complete pantry. These shelves can also be purchased precut at a lumberyard or kitchen furnishings store.

Your local hardware store will usually have a selection of under-cabinet drawers and shelving that can be hung in less than an hour with just a hammer and nails or screws. These storage compartments run the gamut from the usual pull-out type to an assortment of closed cabinets and towel dispensers. They usually sell for about $8 to $10 apiece.

If you already have sufficient storage space, consider its appearance, how it would look to a prospective buyer. If your cabinets are painted, has the paint chipped around the edges? Are grease stains a problem near the knobs? Do old-fashioned or mismatched knobs detract from the appearance of otherwise decent cabinets? All these problems are minor and require very little or no investment to solve. The idea here is to look at your kitchen as objectively as possible. Stand back and examine every square foot with an eye toward finding fault. Remember, you're used to the little blemishes, a prospective buyer will be looking at your home with a much fresher, more critical attitude.

If you've saved some matching paint for cabinets and woodwork, touch up chipped areas with that color. If not, try to match the paint as closely as possible (or repaint just the doors). Any household cleaner that contains ammonia should remove most grease stains from painted surfaces. (Don't use any strong chemicals, they might remove the paint too.) One final hint for quick, inexpensive woodwork improvement: A coat of spray lacquer can make unfinished or stained wood cabinets look like new.

An investment of $10 or less for a set of new doorknobs can make a drastic difference in the appearance of cabinets and drawers. Black wrought iron knobs look wonderful on white cabinet doors; hammered copper and brass knobs go equally well with white or colored cabinets. You'd be surprised what a difference this new hardware can make.

You can dress up plain cabinets with precut door molding from a lumberyard. Centered on the cabinet door (in the shape of a rectangle) and painted to match, or coordinated in another color, these door moldings will unify an otherwise plain kitchen. If you have wallpaper on your kitchen walls and have saved some extra paper, consider papering the space inside the molding.

Kitchen floors that have not been newly re-covered are more than likely stained or torn, or show other signs of not being in the greatest shape. Since so much time is spent in the kitchen and chairs are endlessly being moved around, it is no wonder that the kitchen floor is the first to go, and it is easily noticeable to a prospective buyer.

There are a number of ways you can get around installing a new floor. One simple solution is to put a scatter rug over the part of the floor that is most badly worn. This is usually in front of the sink or under the kitchen table. In either case, a small rug will not look conspicuous and will hide unsightly worn areas.

If the worn spot just happens to be in the middle of the floor or off to the side you might be able to patch the area with a piece of linoleum (or tiles) you may have saved when the floor was installed. With a sharp knife cut a square around the worn area. Be neat or the finished job will look very makeshift. Then, cut a piece from the new flooring. If there is no pattern the job will be simpler, but if there is a pattern make sure you match the new piece to the original floor. Put a piece of cardboard under the hole that has been cut and draw a pencil outline of the area. Cut the patch slightly larger than your outline and see if it fits. If it does, use this piece of cardboard as your pattern. The last step is to take a piece of heavy material, such as linen, cut considerably larger than the size of the patch. Glue your patch firmly to the material. Press the patch into place working the material under the existing linoleum. This will anchor your patch in place. Set a heavy object, such as a book, on the repaired area for a number of hours to let the glue set and the job is complete.

If you feel the floor is too far gone to warrant anything less than a completely new floor, there are some new materials, like indoor/outdoor carpet squares, which allow you to cut and fit your flooring yourself and require no pasting. Another alternative is the press-and-stick tiles that are available at local hardware or lumber dealers. They are easy to cut and install and are usually about half the cost of a professionally installed floor. They won't last as long as professionally installed tile or linoleum, but your kitchen will be much more attractive for months.

Ceramic tile floors have their advantages and disadvantages. If installed properly they will add enormously to the appearance of your kitchen. But installing them yourself is a difficult task and requires a number of days to complete the job. The most inexpensive clay tile (quarry tile) requires a few hours of measuring and setting down before you begin to glue. As many as eight hours may be needed to glue and cut them (with a tile-cutting machine). Twenty-four hours must pass before you can then begin to grout (fill in the cracks with cement). This step again may take five to six hours. You will have to plan on a few more hours of wiping up excess grout before you can seal the floor. The complete job can last four or five days and an amateur can come out with a floor that looks worse than when he started. Unless you are sure of your work, a ceramic floor installation is not a good choice when you plan to sell.

There are a number of ways to make an average kitchen look terrific with a few minor decorating tricks. The most impressive and simplest trick you can use is paint and wallpaper. Painting a small kitchen white will enlarge it, and painting a kitchen with limited sun a bright yellow will give the appearance of sunshine. A cool blue might cut down the glare from a sun-exposed room. Don't use a dark paint or paper if your kitchen is small or has poor light.

Pre-pasted wallpaper for the amateur hanger is available at all wallpaper stores. It's easy to install and far less expensive than regular wallpaper. A pretty floral or geometric print will do wonders for a drab room. Coordinated window coverings will unify the kitchen and make it more appealing. If poor sunlight is a problem try removing window coverings to give a more open feeling.

Lighting plays a vital part in a kitchen. There should be sufficient light in work areas and at least one overhead light. Most people prefer fluorescent lighting because it is inexpensive and sheds bright light over a large area. For softer incandescent light, inexpensive ceiling fixtures can be purchased for as little as $25. If your work areas are lost in shadows, small under-cabinet lighting is a good solution. These units are not expensive and are easy to install.

Check the wall above your stove. If it is covered with grease spots, now is the time to do something about it. If you are planning to paint or paper your kitchen be sure to remove all grease marks before you begin or the paint and wallpaper will not adhere properly. Another possibility for covering the areas behind your stove is inexpensive pre-glued metal tiles. These tiles are available in hardware and paint supply stores and come in a variety of metal finishes such as copper or stainless steel.

One of the important questions any prospective buyer will ask you about your home is whether it has an eat-in kitchen. Many home buyers, especially buyers with two or more children, consider it essential when buying a house. Make an effort to gain some space for a table if there is no space now. One way to create the room is to remove a cabinet unit. It might be worth it even if the space will only permit room for a small table with two chairs. It is more important to have this space than to have an extra cabinet. An unused portion of one wall could have a drop-leaf table which is lifted when the space is needed. Removing just the cabinets under a counter and buying some unfinished stools is another solution to the eat-in kitchen problem. Whichever solution works best in your kitchen, it will definitely add to the salability of your house.

Here are some last minute things you should check before your buyer arrives: First, make sure the kitchen is spotless. Do not leave a stack of dirty dishes in the sink. Cabinets and counter-tops shouldn't be a source of clutter. Remove some of your least-used items and store them temporarily so your counters appear more spacious.

If your kitchen table is not attractive, a bright tablecloth and a vase of flowers or a bowl of fruit is a nice touch. Wax your floor, or at least be sure it's clean, before your buyer arrives. A sweeping may be all that is necessary, but it's important. Make sure all light fixtures are in working order and replace burned-out bulbs.

As a final thought: there is nothing warmer and more delightful than the aroma of fresh-baked bread in the oven.

The Bathrooms

Next to the kitchen, the bathroom is the most important room to prospective buyers. Whether you have a small, old-fashioned "lav" or a modern Japanese extravaganza, your prospect will spend a good deal of time inspecting the condition of these rooms.

If your house is anything larger than a vacation cottage, having only one bath could result in a lost sale. Adding a full second bath could cost $2,000, and this seems to be a great deal of money to invest in a home you are planning to sell. The advantage to a large investment of this kind is that you will probably recover all your costs. This advice is only intended for homes now having only one bath. (Adding a third bath would probably not return more than 80 percent of your investment.)

Most single-bath homes have the bathroom near the bedroom area, therefore the most advantageous spot for a second full or half-bath would probably be near an entrance hall or next to a study/guest room. The least expensive place for a new bath is adjacent to a wet wall (usually found in the kitchen or laundry). You can then avoid the additional costs of new plumbing lines. An extra closet is all the space that is necessary for a guest lav or half-bath. Even a closet as small as 24" x 42" would handle a new corner commode and a wall-hung sink. If you use these types of fixtures and situate the lav next to an existing wet wall you could bring the cost below $1,000, sometimes as low as $500. If you can afford it, a second bath is a most important and salable investment.

Unless you're an experienced plumber, call in an expert to plan and install your new bathroom. A plumber and/or carpenter will advise you on selection of materials, clearance between fixtures and adjacent or facing walls, ability of your walls to support fixtures and access space to pipes for repairs. Plumbers are specialists and their rates are usually high. There are a few points in their favor, however. Having a plumber order your fixtures for you will save some money, since plumbers buy from wholesale suppliers. A local unlicensed plumber or apprentice will usually charge less than a licensed plumber and usually do a good job.

He can even give you expert advice on what kind of fixtures are cheapest and require the least amount of work to install yourself. If you're brave and reasonably handy, a do-it-yourself book on plumbing repairs might give you all the education you need.

If you are interested in remodeling an existing bathroom, you may be able to replace plumbing fixtures yourself, assuming that your pipes are in good condition, and are functioning well. If you regularly do business with a plumber he may agree to purchase the fixtures at his cost as a favor; otherwise shop local discount stores or lumberyards. Either way you will save a considerable amount of money.

There are several types of toilets on the market. Choose the one you buy according to the space you have and the amount of money you want to spend. The "wash-down" toilet is the cheapest, and requires the most upkeep. The reverse-trap and siphon-jet toilets are one step above the wash-down type and work a lot better. The most expensive type is the siphon-vortex toilet. Silent-flush, wall-hang and corner toilets are also available and serve specific needs. If your bathroom will be next to a dining room or kitchen the silent flush certainly has its advantages. Wall-hung models require the least amount of wall space and can be used over concrete floors in a basement or converted garage. If you are using a small area such as a closet, the corner toilet requires the least amount of floor space. Toilets, before installation, can cost from $75 to $200.

Bathroom sinks are far less expensive than toilets and require less installation time and know-how. Besides the standard wall basin, there are numerous shapes and models to choose from. Always remember when buying a sink that it should be strong enough to support your weight if you lean on it. This is especially true of wall-hung models. The most attractive basin is the vanity type which is enclosed in its own cabinet. Aside from being the easiest to install (all the pipes are hidden inside the cabinet) it is the easiest to clean. The most expensive of this type is a one-piece plastic model with an attached backsplash. A medium priced self-rimmed bowl set into a counter-top will certainly be adequate, and is probably the best combination of cost and appeal.

All finishing materials in the bath should be moisture-proof. Ceramic tile is the most frequently used and is attractive, but you can have an appealing bathroom with either vinyl wall covering or enamel paint. If you prefer, wall tiles now come in 4′ x 4′ panels which are glued to the wall with mastic and then grouted. The mastics and grouts that are on the market now are so easy to use that you could tile your bath yourself by following the instructions that come with the panels.

If you have only one bath and cannot afford the expense of a second bathroom, put energy and a little money into making that room stand out. If you are not planning to remodel, at least make sure that your fixtures are in good working order. Is the porcelain badly chipped or cracked? Now is the time to repair these flaws, before your first prospect visits.

If one or more of your bathroom drains gets clogged up periodically, begin *now* to reduce the probability of it happening when a buyer turns on the water. A once-a-day treatment with a chemical drain cleaner compound should offer some help. If the drain is hopelessly blocked, there are a number of steps you can take to undo the clog.

The first thing to do is check the drain plug by removing it and cleaning it out. If this does not solve the problem the trouble is either in the drainpipe itself or in the trap below it. The next thing to try is a plunger. The most effective method is to plug up the overflow hole in the bathtub or sink and remove the drain stopper. Put the plunger over the hole and force it up and down several times. In most cases the pressure will force the blockage through. Run the hot water for a few minutes afterwards to allow the blockage to be carried away.

If none of these procedures work your next alternative is to remove the drain plug located in the U-shaped pipe under the sink or tub. Using a wrench, remove the plug and clean out the blockage. If the trap is also removable, wash it thoroughly with hot water. Use a plumber's snake to clean out the pipes under the fixture.

Clear up leaky faucets before you plan to sell. Again you can do the job yourself by following a few simple steps. The leak is usually caused by a worn washer; leaking around the valve stem means a loose cap nut or deteriorated packing under the nut. Begin by tightening the cap nut. (It's the fitting right below the on/off handle.) If that does not stop the leak you will have to remove the cap nut and replace the packing.

Shut off the water supply to the fixture and then remove the screw that is on the top of the valve handle. You should be able to lift off the handle. Unscrew the cap nut and remove the valve stem. By turning the cap nut over you will be able to determine if the packing has worn out or a new sealing washer is needed. If the packing is worn, winding some string which has been dipped in graphite around the valve stem will stop the leak. (Prepared string is available at hardware stores.) If the sealing ring has deteriorated, a new ring can be purchased at a hardware store.

To repair a dripping faucet follow the same procedure except for removing the packing material. The entire valve assembly must be unscrewed and then removed. At the bottom of the assembly the washer is held in place with a screw. Carefully remove this screw. Lift off the washer and replace with a new one of the same size, and then reassemble the valve stem. Then twist the handle on and off a number of times to set the new washer.

Now turn your attention to the ceramic tile on your bathroom walls. Loose or missing tiles should be replaced. These are glued to the wall with a special tile mastic. Be sure to let the mastic set for at least twenty-four hours before you run the shower or the tiles may fall off from the excess moisture.

Grouting requires a special compound sold in hardware stores (usually made from portland cement). Mix some of the dry compound with water to the consistency of whipped cream and smear over the tile joints with a putty knife. Remove the surplus grouting on the tiles with a wet sponge and wipe with a soft cloth after it dries. You can also get premixed grouting (in tubes) but you're paying extra for the convenience.

Stained or darkened grouting can be cleaned with a stiff toothbrush dipped in household bleach. If this does not remove the stains you may have to scrape away the old grouting and replace it.

Broken caulking around the bathtub can be repaired with a special caulking compound that comes in a tube and is easily squeezed into the cracks around bathtubs and sinks. It's non-yellowing and quite inexpensive.

Epoxy paint and fillers are sold that will hide unsightly scratches and chips in the porcelain of bathtubs and sinks. There is also a refinishing kit for sinks and tubs whose surface has become dull. Painting it on with a special brush restores the gloss to old bathroom fixtures. For a fee (usually less than $75) you can hire a service to refinish all your bathroom fixtures and have them looking sparkling and new.

Rust and water stains can be removed with a solution of household bleach and hot water that is allowed to sit for a few hours. Filling the sink and tub with the solution and letting it sit overnight will usually bleach out the stains.

For less than $20 there are a number of ways to make dramatic improvements in the appearance of your bathroom. Would matching shower curtains and window coverings make your bathroom more attractive? Making your own curtains with colorful bed sheets is the least expensive way. What about adding matching towels and bath mats? There's nothing better to cover an unattractive bathroom floor than inexpensive wall-to-wall bath carpeting that you can cut and install in less than two hours. A new toilet seat will also help, especially if the toilet itself is old. Pre-pasted wallpaper that you can hang in a few hours can also help make a dull bathroom come alive.

For less than a dollar, a rusty shower curtain rod can be covered with plastic rod covers made for this purpose. Inexpensive shelving will hold an assortment of plants (plants grow very well in bathrooms because of the moisture). These cosmetic touches and a few framed pictures may be all you need to make your bathroom more appealing.

If your medicine cabinet is old and worn think about replacing it with a framed mirror that you've refinished yourself. Your bath supplies could then be stored in under-sink cabinets or enclosed wall shelves, or could be removed from the bathroom while your house is being inspected by a prospective buyer.

Lighting seems to be a problem in many bathrooms. One fixture over the mirror is usually not sufficient, and fluorescent lighting in a bathroom gives a deathly pallor. Two incandescent bulbs on each side of the mirror will do the job satisfactorily—unless your bathroom is especially large, then add incandescent light accordingly.

A coat of bright yellow glossy enamel can make a dark room look like it is filled with sunshine. Try to avoid fad colors that may not appeal to all prospective buyers. Remember, too, that unusually colored bathroom fixtures may turn a buyer off (and they cost at least 10 percent more than plain white fixtures).

Bathroom floors are a nuisance. Look at any bathroom floor and you'll see signs of deterioration, especially around tubs and basins. It's the toughest floor to keep clean. (Water damage is usually the culprit.) If you have to replace the bathroom floor, one-piece sheet-vinyl or press-and-stick tiles are the least expensive and they're the easiest to install yourself.

Refer to the master checklist at the end of this chapter before your buyer arrives. And don't forget to put out your best guest towels.

Living room, dining room, family room, bedrooms—altogether will not make up for an unacceptable kitchen or bathroom. So take the money you have to spend on redecorating and spend the bulk of it on those two rooms. The other rooms on the first and second floor cost less to put into salable shape because you are selling space here, rather than more tangible appliances and fixtures.

Space is the key word here. Remember you are selling your space and not your furniture. Rearrange your furniture if necessary to show the *size* of rooms to their fullest advantage. A lot of furniture can make a room look small. Oversize chairs, couches and tables that are out of proportion to the rest of the room should be moved elsewhere (or even stored until you move). Don't forget closets. Buyers will also be looking there to see how much space they offer. A neat, well-arranged closet looks much more spacious than one in which everything has been thrown in haphazardly.

If you have a lot of knick-knacks or your tables are filled with loose items, remove them. You may be hiding some attractive features behind a lot of excess furnishings.

Let's take a walking tour of your house, exactly the

way your prospects will view it, and do a complete inspection room by room.

The Entrance Hall

Your entrance hall or foyer will be the first area your buyer will see. Make it as inviting as possible.

Make sure all door hardware has been polished and the doors are free of handprints. The hardware, hinges, locks, etc., should be in good working condition—your doorbell should ring and hinges should be free of squeaks.

If you have area rugs of any kind they should be cleaned and secure, so a prospective buyer doesn't trip or lift the rug when the door opens. The floor should be polished and free of clutter. There's nothing less appealing than a pile of rubber boots or a bag of trash that you just haven't had the time to remove.

Be sure your hall closet is not overcrowded. Your prospects will be checking the closet and may need the space to hang up their coats. If there is a light in the closet make sure the bulb is not burned out. It's a good idea to have the entryway as light and as cheerful as possible. The walls should be a pastel or subdued print to make the space appear larger and sunlit. Remember, this is where your buyer will get his first impression of the inside of your house. Make the space inviting.

The Living Room

The living room is usually the next room your buyer will see. The easiest way to begin your inspection of the room is to start at the top and work down. Check your ceiling for cracks or stains in the plaster. Cracks can be filled with either premixed or dry spackle that is mixed with water according to package directions. If a hole in the ceiling is quite large it's best to apply the spackling paste in layers, allowing each layer to dry before you apply another. If the crack is narrow but deep, insert a piece of paper for backing and then apply your spackle. A wide hole should be covered with plasterboard first then sealed around the edges with plaster and repainted. Whether you use spackle or plaster, allow it to dry thoroughly before you sand it. The area can then be safely painted to match your ceiling.

Stains on the ceiling can be caused by a number of things, the most common of which is water damage from a leak in the roof or from leaky pipes. Find the cause of the leak and repair it before you repaint.

If the stain is caused by mold growth, wash the surface with an antiseptic solution. Black spots near copper or brass lighting fixtures are caused by lithopone in the paint film and can be remedied by washing the surface and applying a coat of aluminum sealer. Follow this with a coat of zinc oxide paint which will not be affected by the metal fittings. Rust stains should be covered by following the same directions.

The walls are next. Look for cracks and staining and eliminate those problems before repainting the room. Repainting is the single most important thing you can do to improve the complete appearance of your room. (Remember you are selling your space and not your furniture.) Your furniture should still be shown to its best advantage, but more time and money should be spent on the *space* you are showing to a prospective buyer.

Choose your paint colors according to your space. If your room is small and dark, a light, sun-filled white or yellow will give the illusion of space where very little exists. Standing radiators will be less obtrusive if you paint them the same color as the walls. If your walls are dark it will probably take two coats of a lighter color to cover the old paint. As with the rest of the rooms in your house it is better to stick to the lighter pastel shades or white when repainting. Your passion for purple may not inspire your prospective buyer.

If your walls are badly chipped and cracked, or uneven, think of using sand or stucco paints. These cover scarred walls. A stiff brush is needed to slap the paint on the wall, and either a roller or brush is then used to get the desired effect.

If your walls are papered now, check the condition of the seams and around areas such as light switches for lifted corners and frayed edges. These can be glued down with white glue or rubber cement.

Wallpaper does collect dust and dirt. Dust the walls with a soft cloth or dust mop. The brush attachment on your vacuum cleaner is a good way to reach the corners near the ceiling to remove cobwebs and dust. Be careful not to rub the paper. The idea is to brush off the dirt lightly. If the dirt seems to be embedded, you may have to rinse it off with a wet sponge dipped in a detergent solution. Start at the upper corner covering no more than ten square feet at a time or the old glue might become loosened.

Grease spots are usually a problem near switch plates and behind chairs and sofas. Use a rag moistened with mineral spirits or cleaning fluid, then dipped into Fuller's earth and brush over the area. This should eliminate the spots. The excess is then brushed away. You may have to repeat this procedure more than once to completely remove all traces of grease.

Crayon is a little harder to remove. Any excess should be scraped off with a knife, taking care to scrape in one direction only. Cover the area with a mixture of Fuller's earth and mineral spirits and allow it to dry overnight. Brush off the dried powder the next day. Crayon marks should not be removed with cleaning fluid as it tends to spread the crayon and makes complete removal almost impossible.

If the wallpaper is badly torn, faded or simply unattractive, consider removing it, or (as a shortcut) just paint over it. By sanding those areas that are torn and sanding the seams flat, only an expert with an eagle eye would be able to tell that there was wallpaper under the paint. Of course, flat paint cannot be used over flocked or raised patterns, or on moiré or fabric-faced papers. Try one of the textured paints for these walls. Do not be too concerned if the paper appears to pucker while you are painting. It will shrink back to flat when the paint has dried.

As a temporary first-aid measure, hang a few pictures over worn areas. It is not likely that buyers will look behind pictures to see if there are any marks.

Be sure your windows are clean throughout the house, especially if you have a view to sell. Curtains should be fresh and used to complement the windows rather than overshadow them.

Decorative window treatments can be a help, if your window placement is bad. A window that is poorly positioned in the middle of the room can be made to appear larger by extending the curtains a few feet on either side of the window. A small room can give the appearance of more space by covering one wall entirely with draperies of the same color as on the window. Soften the hard lines of a square room with tiebacks or flounced valances. And if the view is spectacular from your living room window by all means leave the curtains open when your prospects arrive.

Play up the important features of a room. Your fireplace should be cleaned and free of loose ash. In cool weather, have a fire going when your guests arrive. The brick should be cleaned and the mantel cleared of odds and ends. A fireplace is an important asset and should be given careful attention. Built-in shelves will be shown to their best advantage if they're free of clutter. Closed cabinets should be cleaned to emphasize spaciousness.

Carpeting should be vacuumed and spot-cleaned with a commercial rug cleaner. Badly worn wall-to-wall carpeting should not be replaced. The carpet you choose may not be to everyone's taste and you won't recover its cost if you have to leave it when you move. A more practical solution is to remove the carpet completely and clean or refinish the floor under it. If the floor is wood a careful check should be made to make sure the boards are not weak or creaky. If you do find some creaks they can be fixed by driving finishing nails (nails without heads) at opposite angles through the boards into the supporting joists.

Sanding and refinishing wood floors will present problems if you are working in a room filled with furniture. It is best to remove at least the larger pieces while you work. Cover the furniture in this and the adjoining rooms because the sawdust from the sander travels far and will invade every room in your house. Plan floor work at least a week before your first buyer arrives (to give yourself time to dust off all the excess sawdust).

A word of caution when using a commercial floor sander: Do not smoke. One spark could ignite the cloud of sawdust and cause an explosion.

Floor sanders can be rented from hardware stores, lumberyards or rental agencies. The machines are quite heavy and take some getting used to but they can be mastered. Be sure you get two or three grades of sanding discs when you rent your machine.

The first step is a rough sanding with the heaviest grade of sandpaper, followed by a second sanding with the next grade of paper. It's a good idea to start sanding in the far corner of the room so beginners errors are less obvious. The third sanding is done with the finest grade of sandpaper and should result in a completely smooth finish. Two coats of stain should be applied and allowed to dry at least eight hours between coats. A minimum of three coats of plastic finish such as Fabulon or polyurethane is recommended for a tough, hard surface that will never need waxing. Do not walk on the plastic finish for at least twenty-four hours to avoid footprints.

As you look around the room, try to see it as your prospective buyer would. Check for defects you might have overlooked because of your familiarity with your house. What is the general character of the room? Is it warm and cozy? Is it cool and elegant? Stick to one look and play it to the fullest with paint and paper, positioning of furniture and lighting. Don't have your horseshoe-shaped couch standing in a major traffic area. If your prospects have to walk around furniture to get into the room, the space will appear smaller than it actually is. Store unsightly large pieces of furniture until you move.

Now is the time to call a rummage shop or have a

garage sale to get rid of all the odds and ends you've accumulated over the years. They get in the way in the house you are selling and are an additional expense when you move. The Salvation Army or Goodwill will pick up large pieces, as long as they are in reasonable or salvageable condition.

For $25 or less you can add some "magic touches" like colorful throw pillows, fresh green plants or a large vase of cut flowers. Inexpensive framed prints add color and space to a large expanse of wall. If the room is dark during the day a few five-dollar table lamps will add interest and brightness.

Family rooms and studies should receive the same attention you gave to your living room. But remember, hobby supplies, games and papers had best be stored out of sight.

The checklist at the end of the chapter should be used to review those areas.

The Bedrooms

Bedrooms are frequently the most neglected rooms in a house, since families spend very little time in their bedrooms during the day. You rarely, if ever, entertain guests in your bedroom. So these rooms seem to get the short end of the stick when it comes to decorating and remodeling.

Look carefully around the room. The ever-present collection of lotions, sprays, pins and odds and ends on top of the dresser will have to be put away. The pile of bills on the night table should be stored in a drawer. The bedspread should be taken out of the closet and put on the bed. (The bed should be made every day that you expect buyers to come.) Take down the curtains and wash and iron them. Be sure dirty clothes are stored in the laundry hamper and not on the chair or bed. Remove the excess furniture that gives the room a crowded look. Remember, as with the living room, the space is what you are selling, not your beautiful pine bedroom suite.

A thorough cleaning is absolutely necessary. Vacuum the rug and remove any stains. Make sure the furniture is dust free. Try to give the impression that the house is easy to take care of.

Give the ceiling and walls the same treatment you might have given the living room. That is, repair cracks in the ceiling and walls, repair torn wallpaper, repaint if necessary.

A bedroom is a retreat of sorts. It's important that it appear as pleasant and inviting as possible.

Children's rooms present another kind of problem, especially if you do not have a separate playroom. Toys take complete control of a room and eventually overpower the space. Store larger pieces in the garage or attic until the house is sold. Now is the time to clear away out-grown toys. You will have less to move after you sell and the room will be neater and more spacious. Whatever toys cannot be stored or given away should be arranged on shelves or in cabinets. Do not let your children make a shambles of the house while you are trying to sell it. It will give the buyers the idea that you allow your children to be careless about all your property. Try to remove all stains, crayon marks, etc. on the walls of children's rooms.

Do not use your children's room as the focus of your painting talents. Now is not the time to paint the walls a bright red or neon blue. As with the other rooms, a white or pastel color is preferred here. There will be no guarantee that the new owner will have children, or appreciate the dark walls he or she may have to repaint with two or three coats of paint.

If the wooden floors in your child's room are badly scratched from toy trucks and blocks you can salvage them with a simple procedure: Use a pad of fairly coarse steel wool that has been saturated with gasoline or other solvent. Rub the finish off in the direction of the wood grain. Fill the scratches with wood filler, colored to match the floor. When the filler dries, sand it smooth and clean the area with a rag dipped in solvent. You can then refinish the area by brushing on diluted shellac varnish, or (if the floor is oil varnished) ordinary varnish diluted with turpentine.

Linoleum tiles in a child's room get a lot of abuse. If one or more tiles are curled or damaged they can be removed by steaming them with an ordinary steam iron. The steam will cause the glue to melt and then the bad tiles can be lifted out. Replace them with new tiles of the same type or use a good tile lifted from a corner of the room where it cannot be seen or missed.

An infant's room should be kept fresh-smelling with room deodorizers. If possible keep your diaper pail in the bathroom or out of sight completely.

Second and third bedrooms or guest rooms deserve the same attention you give to the master bedroom. Use the checklist at the end of the chapter when inspecting those rooms.

The Basement

Problem basements are signs of serious trouble to any prospective buyer. A damp or wet basement will tell your prospect a great deal about what he is going to get for his money—extra headaches or extra space. Serious foundation and drainage problems may exist when your basement appears wet or damp. You must rectify (or at least mask) the situation before you intend to sell.

First and foremost you must *dry* a damp basement. Many can be dried by simply wrapping cold water pipes which will eliminate the condensation of water. If the pipes feel wet and the floor under them is damp, condensation has taken place. Buy commercial pipe wrapping at a hardware store and wrap all pipes that feel wet when you touch them. This simple operation may be all you have to do to dry your damp basement.

If the dampness can be felt on the walls of your basement, a dehumidifier is the simplest and the fastest way to remedy the situation. Keep it going until the basement dries. Not only will it remove the water problem but it should also eliminate the musty odors that accompany wet basements.

Unventilated clothes driers are another source of condensation on basement walls and floors. (The moisture released by your drier has to go somewhere.) Extend your drier's ventilation pipe out a window. Then use a dehumidifier to remove the excess dampness.

Unfortunately, there are more serious problems that might be causing basement dampness: Cracks in the floor or in the basement walls, leaks from pipes that go through the walls, plugged-up drains and leaks in basement windows and the most serious of all, poor drainage around the foundation.

Tackle the least complicated problems first. If there are cracks in the walls or floor they must be filled. Ordinary cement paints will not be effective in keeping water out. You must use special waterproofing materials to get satisfactory results. One of these is a heavy-duty powdered cement that is mixed with water and applied liberally with a stiff brush. Latex or oil-based paint will have to be removed first to make the wall porous. (A simple test to see if the wall is porous is to splash some water on the wall and see if it soaks in or runs off. If it does soak in you are ready to cement—after the splashed water dries.) If the water runs off you must remove all old surface materials. Chip out all loose debris in the cracks and holes and fill with quick-setting cement. After that dries, completely cover the area with your waterproofing material.

A more expensive but faster way to handle this problem is to prepare an epoxy resin in two parts that is mixed just before use. The walls need not be cleaned of surface paint, but you should fill all cracks before you apply the material. You may need to apply the resin only along the joints where the walls meet the floor. Two coats are required to completely halt seepage.

If the basement floor is a major source of dampness and you can find no obvious cause, try this simple test: Place a sheet of waterproof building paper or heavy aluminum foil over a portion of the floor. Weigh it down with a heavy object and leave it in position for a few days. If the underside of the paper is damp after the elapsed time, moisture from the ground below is rising in the form of a vapor right through the foundation. You will need to coat the floor with a sealer of vapor-barrier masonry paint. Another, more expensive solution is to cover the floor with waterproof building paper and then build a new floor above it.

If you have a really bad water problem on your basement floor, a sump pump may be the only solution. You will have to dig a small hole in the basement floor near the main water source. Line the hole with cement and have the electric sump pump installed. The service fee usually runs from $50 to $75, in addition to the cost of the pump.

There are a few quick easy solutions to water problems that originate outside your house. Check the drainpipes to see if they are clogged. If they are, water may be breaking through the walls and into the basement. Make sure your roof drains, or leaders, are directed *away* from the house and that there is a concrete splash block directly below these drains to absorb water. Be sure the ground slopes away from the house around the foundation so water is not being funneled directly into the basement.

If none of these precautions eliminate the water seepage, you definitely have a serious water problem and your only alternative is to call in a waterproofing expert. He may have to dig a trench completely around your house and lay in a tile pipe to catch the groundwater and carry it away. The exterior wall surfaces may also have to be waterproofed. This procedure is expensive, but if you have a serious water problem, your house will be far less salable without this "cure."

Chronic water problems may have left your walls covered with fungus stains. The growths are dark in color and disfigure painted surfaces. There are two types of fungus growth, one dark gray or black and the other bluish-green. The gray or black fungus is harder to remove because it penetrates the surface and leaves spores that will reappear even after the growth seems to have been removed. It is advisable in this case to use a special fungicide solution that will destroy the spores. The bluish-green type of fungus can easily be wiped off the surface with a damp cloth. A wall painted with gloss or enamel paint is less likely to be attacked by fungus growth.

All evidence of water stains should at least be covered or your buyer will instantly know that there has been water damage. If you've repaired cracks in the ceilings and floor you may have to repaint to hide the evidence of the damage. Floor tiles that have lifted because of flooding should be replaced or the floor should be completely recovered.

If you use your basement as your prime storage area it may be a good idea to store the bulkier items elsewhere until after you sell your house. You'll find it easier to clean when there is less clutter and your buyer will be better able to judge the amount of storage space he is getting.

If your laundry area is in the basement try to make it as inviting as possible. Maximum lighting should be installed so that the buyer doesn't feel he or she has to go into a cave to do their laundry. An inexpensive piece of linoleum in front of the washer and drier is not only attractive but practical, if you have a cement floor. It is easier to keep clean and dropped clothes will not have to be rewashed. Try to remove clean laundry as soon as it is finished. Piles of laundry are not only unattractive but take up space.

The basement should be swept and the floor free of excess clutter. Be sure mops and other cleaning equipment are not blocking the stairway to the basement. The stair's railing should be tightened to support any weight that might be put on it, and any loose carpet runners should be tacked down.

Keeping the basement windows clean helps your basement look brighter. Cracked or missing windowpanes should be replaced not only as a fuel-saving measure, but because they detract from the appearance of the room.

Any serious defects in your heating system should be handled by a heating expert before you plan to sell. Problems such as inadequate distribution of heat, clogged fuel lines, or heavy rust damage are not do-it-yourself repair jobs.

There are a few simple ways to temporarily mask heating problems. Discolorations on the walls around heat outlets indicate that the heating plant is inefficiently using fuel. Repainting those areas will conceal the inefficiency.

The main filter installed in a warm-air furnace should be taken out and cleaned. (Your fuel bills may be lowered 10 percent by removing this accumulated dirt.) The filter is found at the side or the back of the furnace and can be just lifted off and brushed or vacuumed clean. If the filter is permanent, as on some newer models, simply wash it off with sudsy water and replace the adhesive coating that traps dirt.

In the rest of the house, be sure warm-air ducts are free from debris, and grilles are not covered with rugs or any other barriers.

All moving parts in a hot-water-system furnace should be lubricated with SAE Number 20 oil. Remember, to turn off both the motor and the pump before you begin any furnace work.

If you discover a foul odor emanating from your air ducts, you may have dead mice nestled in there. You will have to have the ducts opened to remove the vermin.

The Garage

When structurally sound, the garage is a distinct selling point, not only as a place for family cars, but as a haven for the tons of junk that every family accumulates over the years. (And drags around with them from house to house.)

This is the time to do a complete cleaning out of all the unwanted furniture and old bikes that have been sitting in your garage. All large pieces should be either stored elsewhere or removed so the storage space you are offering can be fully appreciated.

Assuming that your garage needs only an afternoon's worth of cleaning up there are some points you should consider when you begin your cleanup. The workbench area should be neatly arranged with all tools hung on pegboard or stored in cabinets. Garden equipment such as rakes and shovels should also be hung on hooks to allow for more floor space. Open shelving is a good idea for all paint cans, storage boxes and odds and ends. Keep the garage floor free of oil and grease puddles.

Be sure all light fixtures are operating, especially if there is a work area in the garage. Electric door openers should be operating since you will probably have to demonstrate their effectiveness to your prospective buyer. Be certain that door springs are lubricated and working effectively.

If oil spots are a problem on the floor of the garage, they can be eliminated with a bag of kitty litter. The litter absorbs oil and it can then be swept away. There are special mixtures sold for removing oil stains but they are far more expensive than kitty litter and do no better job.

All separate storage areas should receive the same cleaning treatment as your main garage space. This includes storage sheds on your property and your attic.

If you have allowed your garage to become an eyesore, it may be to your advantage to level it completely and replace it with a carport or car shelter.

The following pages contain checklists for the areas of your home discussed in this chapter. They've been included to help you make a detailed inspection and repair record as you prepare your house for sale.

CHECKLIST FOR LANDSCAPING

LAWN
Lawn in good condition   _____
Grass mowed   _____
Edges trimmed around   _____
    walks   _____
    driveways   _____
    trees   _____
    fences   _____

TREES
Dead branches pruned   _____
Dead trees removed   _____

PLANTINGS
Dead shrubs removed   _____
Dead shrubs replaced   _____
Overgrown shrubs pruned   _____

CHECKLIST FOR EXTERIOR

HOUSE
Recently painted   _____
Free of flaking paint   _____
Gutters free of rust   _____
Gutters recently painted   _____
Exterior lights operating   _____
Missing shingles replaced _____
Doorbell working   _____
Exterior Brass polished   _____
Windows
    Cracked panes replaced _____
    Trim recently painted   _____
    Work freely

DRIVEWAY
Resurfaced _____
Potholes patched _____
Recently sealed _____
Pebbles smoothed _____
Pebbles weeded _____

PATIOS
Wood stained or painted _____
Fencing secure _____
No standing water _____

CHECKLIST FOR KITCHEN

Sink free of cracks _____
Sink free of stains _____
No dripping faucets _____
Refrigerator defrosted _____

Appliances in good working order _____
Missing floor tiles replaced _____
Walls free of grease stains _____
Counter-tops cleared _____
Pantry and cabinets
    Neatly arranged _____
    Hardware replaced _____
    Excess storage removed _____
    Grease stains removed _____
    Cabinet doors repainted _____

CHECKLIST FOR BATHROOM #1

Sink stains removed _____
Leaky faucets repaired _____
Stains removed from grouting _____
All joints caulked _____
Broken or missing tiles replaced _____
All fixtures operating _____
Wallpaper repaired _____
Recently painted _____
Floors cleaned _____
New shower curtain _____
All supplies stored _____
Guest towels out _____

CHECKLIST FOR BATHROOM #2

Sink stains removed _____
Leaky faucet repaired _____
Stains removed from grouting _____
All joints caulked _____

Broken or missing tiles replaced   ———
All fixtures operating   ———
Wallpaper repaired   ———
Recently painted   ———
Floors cleaned   ———
New shower curtain   ———
All supplies stored   ———
Guest towels out   ———

CHECKLIST FOR ENTRANCE HALL

Doorbell operating   ———
Door recently painted   ———
Door brass polished   ———
Hardware operating   ———
Hinges oiled   ———
Broken hinges replaced   ———
Outside bulb replaced   ———
Entryway lights operating   ———
Floors cleaned   ———
Rugs cleaned and secure   ———
Curtains washed and ironed   ———
Windows washed   ———
Closet light operating   ———
Closet cleaned out   ———
Walls recently painted   ———
Wallpaper repaired   ———
Ceiling and wall cracks repaired   ———

CHECKLIST FOR LIVING ROOM

Cracks in ceiling and walls repaired   ———
Water stains covered   ———

Walls recently painted   ———
Wallpaper repaired   ———
Woodwork repainted   ———
Windows washed   ———
Cracked or missing panes replaced   ———
Curtains washed and ironed   ———
Windows operating freely   ———
Draperies open to show view   ———
Floor waxed   ———
Floor refinished   ———
Carpets clean and secure   ———
Furniture positioned to show space   ———
Large pieces stored elsewhere   ———

CHECKLIST FOR DINING ROOM

Cracks in ceiling and walls repaired   ———
Water stains covered   ———
Wallpaper repaired   ———
Woodwork repainted   ———
Windows washed   ———
Cracked or missing panes replaced   ———
Curtains washed and ironed   ———
Windows operating freely   ———
Draperies open to show view   ———
Floor waxed   ———
Floor refinished   ———
Carpets clean and secure   ———
Furniture positioned to show space   ———
Large pieces stored elsewhere   ———
Tablecloth fresh   ———

CHECKLIST FOR FAMILY ROOM/STUDY

Cracks in ceiling and walls repaired   ———

Water stains covered   ———

Wallpaper repaired   ———

Woodwork repainted   ———

Windows washed   ———

Cracked or missing panes replaced   ———

Curtains washed and ironed   ———

Windows operating freely   ———

Draperies open to show view   ———

Floor waxed   ———

Floor refinished   ———

Carpets clean and secure   ———

Furniture positioned to show space   ———

Large pieces stored elsewhere   ———

Hobby supplies put away   ———

CHECKLIST FOR BEDROOM #1

Cracks in ceiling and walls repaired   ———

Water stains covered   ———

Wallpaper repaired   ———

Woodwork repainted   ———

Windows washed   ———

Cracked or missing panes replaced   ———

Curtains washed and ironed   ———

Windows operating freely   ———

Draperies open to show view   ———

Floor waxed   ———

Floor refinished   ———

Carpets clean and secure   ———

Furniture positioned to show space   ———

Large pieces stored elsewhere _____
Bed made _____
Night table supplies stored _____
Laundry put away _____

CHECKLIST FOR BEDROOM #2

Cracks in ceiling and walls repaired _____
Water stains covered _____
Wallpaper repaired _____
Woodwork repainted _____
Windows washed _____
Cracked or missing panes replaced _____
Curtains washed and ironed _____
Windows operating freely _____
Draperies open to show view _____
Floor waxed _____
Floor refinished _____
Carpets clean and secure _____
Furniture positioned to show space _____
Large pieces stored elsewhere _____
Bed made _____
Night table supplies stored _____
Laundry put away _____

CHECKLIST FOR CHILDREN'S BEDROOM

Cracks in ceiling and walls repaired _____
Water stains covered _____
Wallpaper repaired _____
Woodwork repainted _____
Windows washed _____

Cracked or missing panes replaced   ————
Curtains washed and ironed   ————
Windows operating freely   ————
Draperies open to show view   ————
Floor waxed   ————
Floor refinished   ————
Carpets clean and secure   ————
Furniture positioned to show space   ————
Large pieces stored elsewhere   ————
Bed made   ————
Laundry put away   ————
Unused toys cleared out   ————
All toys shelved or put away   ————
Floor free from clutter   ————

CHECKLIST FOR BASEMENT

Cracks in ceiling and walls repaired   ————
No evidence of water penetration   ————
Dampness removed   ————
Cold water pipes covered   ————
Dehumidifier installed   ————
Sump pump installed   ————
No musty odors   ————
Drains cleared   ————
Furnace cleaned   ————
Storage neatly arranged   ————
Excess storage removed   ————
Floor swept   ————
Light fixtures operating   ————
Laundry area clean and light   ————
Stairway free of cleaning equipment   ————
Handrail secure   ————
Stairway runners secure and clean   ————

CHECKLIST FOR GARAGE

Excess storage removed ———
Floor swept and clear ———
Tools stored neatly on pegboard ———
Paint supplies stored on shelves ———
Garden equipment on hooks ———
Workbench area well lit ———
Light fixtures operating ———
Oil spots removed from floor ———
Door operating ———
Door lubricated ———
Cracked or missing windowpanes replaced ———
Electric door opener operable ———

CHAPTER

2

How to Price Your House to Sell

Setting the asking price of your house is the most important decision you'll reach when you decide to sell. Overprice and your house may sit on the market for months, losing most of your potential buyers. Underpricing may lead to a quick sale—and a loss of thousands of dollars. In addition to losing substantial money on the quick sale, underpricing almost always makes house buyers wonder what may be wrong with your house.

There are several steps we'll be discussing in this section on pricing. Follow this process and you'll be taking the problem in hand, step-by-step.

The first thing to do is establish the fair market value for your house. That's the price your house should command based on objective, realistic conditions right now.

Most homeowners have a tendency to inflate the value of their houses. It's not until some of these homes remain on the market for months that a homeowner lowers his sights. A highly overpriced home quickly builds a reputation as being untouchable. The longer it remains on the market the more likely it will be left there.

Most buyers will be financing your house with a loan from a bank. With the loan comes the bank's appraisal. If the bank appraises your house for less than your selling price your buyer may have to put up more cash than he or she planned and consequently may be forced to back out of the sale. Aside from the other disappointments, you will have wasted precious selling time.

It is essential for you to determine the fair market value for your house. You can then establish your minimum price and your asking price, the fair market value being what you hope to reach by negotiation. You can then close the sale and turn your market value into your market price.

If you have some money to spend, call in a professional appraiser (one listed as a member of the American Institute of Real Estate Appraisers). You can find these private appraisers listed in the yellow pages of your telephone directory. The fee is usually between $50 and $100 depending on the size of your home.

There are several advantages to using a professional appraiser. You've *lived* in your house and you don't have much of a purely objective feeling about it. It's the trained appraiser's job to determine the fair market value based on purely professional considerations. The appraiser's advice will be valuable when you want answers to questions about the special features in your house. How valuable is your tennis court or formal rose garden? Non-athletic buyers may consider a tennis court a nuisance because of the required upkeep. The appraiser familiar with the existing market conditions will be helpful here.

There are many kinds of appraisers, but you should be interested only in an *independent, experienced, professional, residential real estate* appraiser. Real estate appraisers tend to specialize. Some restrict their work only to commercial property or farm appraisals.

An independent real estate appraiser appraises property for a fee. He or she is not associated with a real estate office or brokerage firm. Look for an appraiser who has worked for several years in your vicinity and specializes in appraising residential property.

A professional appraiser uses three methods to appraise property. In some cases he will incorporate all three when making a judgment or choose one or two that will best suit your property.

The sales-price method is based on the assumption that the property is worth what it will sell for. The appraiser will research the market for information about the sales of similar properties and then compare the qualities of the different properties to determine the market value of yours. This method seems to be the most accurate for determining the value of residential homes, because it concentrates on the real estate market in your neighborhood.

The reproduction or replacement method is used in combination with the sales-price method. Reproduction or replacement is done by estimating the value of the land, adding this to the cost of reproducing the improvements, and then subtracting the depreciation. The result of this calculation is the fair market value of your house and property.

The third method, the *income capitalization method* is normally used only on rental properties like commercial buildings or apartment houses. Since it's unlikely that your home is a true income-producing property this method is not pertinent.

There are ways you can get a good idea of the fair market value of your home without a professional appraiser. Begin by setting a bottom limit—the absolute minimum price you'll accept for your house. It's not what your house is worth, but a price below which you will not be willing to negotiate.

If you're selling your house and purchasing a new home you will probably be depending on the cash from the sale of your present home to purchase your new home. Remember, there are certain additional expenses you will have to incur as part of the sale of your present house. These are: an appraiser, if you hire a professional; advertising; general repairs to the house; lawyer's fees; and closing costs. These costs must be added to your minimum cash needs. If you end up using a real estate agent to sell your house, plan on an additional expense of from 4 to 7 percent of the selling price of the house.

Once you've set your bottom price limit, put yourself in the place of a prospective buyer. If you were in the market for a house in your neighborhood, how much would you be willing to pay for it? Would you pay more than the price similar houses in your neighborhood were selling for?

So let's start by "shopping" your neighborhood. You might have looked at other homes before you bought your house. You probably compared features, location, the size of the property, and the prices before you made up your mind. But that may have been years ago. Your research is dated.

Ask your old and new neighbors what they paid for their houses. If you have a friend who's a real estate agent, pump him or her for information. They are usually on top of the pricing trends in town. Take a ride through your own and similar neighborhoods, noting

"For Sale" signs. Call a few of the most similar homes and pose as a potential buyer. Ask what they're asking for their house and what features it offers. You should be able to pick up a pattern of asking prices in your neighborhood in relation to the size of the house, the amount of property it has and any important extras that raise the price.

You can also find out the price range in your neighborhood by calling up the lending institution that is carrying your mortgage. They usually keep a record of recent purchases made and may give you the information you want.

Check classified ads to inspect the comparable homes that are for sale in your area.

Unless it's the dead of winter, a slow market, with few homes for sale, is a good sign for you. The demand probably exceeds the supply of homes and your home may command a premium price.

Another valuable way to get your market information is to inspect homes with a real estate broker. Call (if you don't plan to buy another home in your area) and pose as a potential buyer. See as many homes as possible that are like your house.

Once you've arrived at the fair market value of your house, with or without the help of professionals, you've decided the price your house *should* command. If you've followed the decorating/repair suggestions from Chapter 1, you should be able to get 10 percent or more above that price. With this in mind, let's discuss the specific pricing of your house.

First, take an objective look at your improvements. If you've installed crystal bathroom faucets, don't expect the buyer to return that $500 investment. As a general rule, discount the value of "extravagant" improvements. The best thing to do with expensive or antique hardware items is to take them with you and replace them with ordinary hinges, faucet knobs or whatever.

Unusual improvements, like a built-in aquarium or small greenhouse, may lower the value of your property. If you leave them they require upkeep. If you remove them you leave an awkward space that needs filling. Be objective when you evaluate what the *average* buyer may consider an improvement or a detriment to the property.

Some improvements depreciate in value the day after you have them installed. Tennis courts and swimming pools, for instance. The money you spent five years ago may not be worth $15,000 added to the price of your house, even though it could cost at least that much to build a new tennis court or pool.

There are certain extras that usually are included in your asking price. As a general rule, anything that has been *installed* on the premises becomes part of the property unless stated otherwise in the final sales contract. It's important to realize what could be considered "part of the property."

All lighting fixtures, storm and screen windows, built-in bookcases and cabinets, indoor and outdoor shutters, window valances, garbage disposals, venetian blinds, shades and TV antennas are considered part of the property. If any of these items are to be moved with you, you must make your intentions clear to the buyer. When itemizing the installed extras you may want to take with you, don't overlook outdoor accessories like built-in or gas barbeques, picnic tables, basketball backboard or volleyball net. If the prize rosebush you've been nurturing for the last ten years is going with you, make this clear to your prospective buyer.

Heavy, but movable items such as washers and driers, air conditioners, kitchen appliances and basement freezers are some of the items you may wish to sell to the prospective buyer. These are not always included in the price of the house, and it is up to you to decide whether to include them as extras or as part of the package.

There are some items that aren't normally considered part of the property, but can be used as strong selling points.

The beautiful draperies that you had dyed to match the carpet in the living room may be of no use to you in your new house. Yet they might be useful as a sales clincher when you have your buyer ripe for the sale.

Things like custom window shades, fireplace screens, mirrored walls—anything that has been tailor-made for your house—can be pointed out as an added incentive to the buyer, but it is unlikely that you will be able to remove any of these things to your new home.

Itemize your home's extras by walking from room to room recording all the details in a notebook. Then decide what you can afford to leave, what you want to sell and what you want to take with you.

After you've established the minimum price you have to get for your house and the fair market value (hopefully higher than the minimum price you need) you have to determine your asking price. The most important thing to remember is that the real estate market is a bargaining market. Your buyer will probably expect to negotiate on the price of your house. He doesn't expect to pay the asking price unless your house is an incredible bargain. Leave some room between the fair market value (that you hope to get) and your asking price.

Adding 5 to 10 percent to the market value should give you sufficient room for bargaining. The spread varies from city to city, but you should have a feeling for your area by pricing similar homes.

After you've established your asking price, take a firm stand and don't indicate to *anyone* that you're willing to take less. You'll have plenty of chances to negotiate with prospective buyers who are really interested in your house, or you will be emphasizing to the buyer that he must negotiate. This is your price and you aim to get it.

CHAPTER

3

How to Market and Show Your House Without a Broker

First, ask yourself, should you try to sell your house without a broker? A real estate broker is supposedly a professional whose career is spent selling homes in your area. It is a time-consuming, skill-demanding job.

If you use a licensed real estate broker, you are required by law to pay his or her commission when your house is sold. The fee is usually between 4 and 7 percent. A 6 percent commission on a $35,000 house is $2,100!

Is the service of a trained real estate agent worth what could amount to several hundred dollars? If you want to avoid the time and energy necessary to price and sell your own house, this service may indeed be worth it. Most brokers are part of a multiple listing service and they can almost assure you'll get lots of lookers, if not buyers.

You'll still have to put your house in salable shape, and maintain it in viewing condition, but a broker spares you the need to traipse all over the house with strangers many times a day.

Most home sellers don't consider themselves expert

at selling real estate. Agents know this—and use it as a selling point when offering their services. But if you can spare a little time to learn the "tricks" of house selling, you can become a very effective agent. And you have one advantage over a real estate agent. You know your house better than anyone else. You are probably the best equipped, from living experience, to emphasize the good features and smooth over the disadvantages of your own home. It's a matter, really, of putting yourself in the frame of mind of a home seller. You can't reveal feelings of hurt or defensiveness when fielding complaints from prospective buyers. Once you develop a bit of a thick skin about your home, you'll be well on your way to a successful sale.

There's another benefit when you sell directly. Buyer's tend to think they're in on a bargain as soon as they see that no agent is involved. Some buyers feel that they might even be able to put one over on the "amateur" who's selling his own home. With a few intelligent selling techniques at your disposal you can have this kind of buyer eating out of your hand.

Whether or not you use a real estate agent, you're well advised, before putting your house on the market, to line up a good real estate attorney. The function of this lawyer will be outlined in more detail later.

There are four steps to follow when you proceed on your own to sell your house. They are: listing, presentation, negotiation and closing.

Listing means preparing a selling sheet on your house —a capsule description of your property that lists all essential information about your house. It's an important selling tool and will give you, quickly at hand, all the basic information a prospective buyer will want to know about your house.

When completed, you should make enough copies

to give one to each interested buyer. Besides using it to compare to other homes the buyer may have visited, it will help the prospect remember your house weeks after the visit.

The listing sheet should be prepared with great care. In addition to its value as a selling tool, a misrepresentation may result in a lawsuit for you. All the information in your listing sheet must be completely accurate.

A sample listing sheet appears at the end of this chapter, along with one blank sheet which you can duplicate.

To prepare your sheet, follow this procedure:

1. Try to find the listing sheet you may have saved when you bought your house. Collect the following information from your household files: tax and utility bills, the surveyor's map, floor plan, or your builder's advertising brochures.

2. Check the details requested on the blank listing sheet at the end of this chapter and survey your house carefully for the information required.

3. After you've double-checked all your data, type or print it neatly in the blank spaces.

4. It's helpful to have a photograph of your house. You don't need a professional photograph, just a black-and-white snapshot taken from the street in front of your house. Take several pictures from spots which show the best angle of your house in relation to your property. Select the best print and attach it to the space provided on your sheet.

5. Once you have completed the listing sheet, have 100 to 200 copies made. Your printing bill should be less than $25.

Refer to the blank listing sheet at the end of this chapter. This is what the spaces should contain: The center portion to the right of the heading "For Sale By Owner" is for entering your name, residence phone and business phone. If you do not want to be called at work, leave this space blank. The section to the right of the owner's name is to be used as "advertising space." Insert excerpts from your newspaper advertisement (more on creating an ad later). Try not to repeat the highly detailed information that will be used on the lower part of the listing sheet unless they are extraordinary features really worth emphasizing. Here are a couple of examples of how to fill this "advertising space":

SECLUDED WOODED LOT	COMPLETELY REFURBISHED COLONIAL
Completely modern kitchen on 3-acre parklike setting.	Ideal family house located on cul-de-sac. Large oaks in quiet setting.

In the space below the heading, fill in the name of the community, the total number of rooms, the number of bedrooms, the number of baths, and the asking price. The lower portion is filled in as follows:

STYLE: State whether your house is ranch, colonial, Cape Cod, English, Tudor, traditional, contemporary, split, raised ranch, Dutch Colonial, cottage, etc.

CONSTRUCTION: Indicate stone, brick, clapboard, brick veneer, aluminum siding, cedar, redwood, frame, or a combination of more than one.

AGE: The age of your house. If you are uncertain, approximate age will do.

LOT SIZE: Acreage or dimensions of the lot, such as 180' x 90'. If you're uncertain, put down approximate size, such as ⅓ acre. (One acre is 43,560 sq. ft.)

SQUARE FEET: This is the square footage of living space, not including the garage, attic or basement, unless the basement has living space such as a family room.

LIVING ROOM: Dimensions of your living room to the nearest foot.

DINING ROOM: Dimensions of your dining room.

FAMILY ROOM: Indicate the dimensions.

BEDROOM #1: Give the dimensions of your bedroom and indicate which is the master bedroom.

BEDROOM #2: Exact dimensions.

BEDROOM #3: Exact dimensions.

KITCHEN: Dimensions of your kitchen.

BREAKFAST ROOM: Give dimensions.

BASEMENT: Explain whether finished or unfinished or if such things as laundry facilities are available there.

GARAGE: Indicate one- or two-car and attached or detached.

CLOSETS: Indicate number of closets and how many are walk-ins.

PATIO: Type of covering, such as cement, stone, brick. Also any special features like a built-in gas grill.

FIREPLACE: Number of fireplaces and their location.

CARPETS: Rooms that have wall-to-wall carpeting and age of carpets.

DRAPES: Indicate which rooms will have drapes left by the owner.

HEAT: Type of heating system, whether forced hot-air, electric, oil, etc.

AIR-CONDITIONING: Number of units you will leave or central system.

DISHWASHER: The age of the dishwasher and brand name.

DISPOSAL: Brand name and age.

STOVE: Brand name and age.

CITY WATER: Yes or no.

SEWER: Yes or no.

PROPERTY TAXES: Amount you pay annually.

SCHOOLS: Elementary and junior or senior high schools in your district.

The empty spaces at the bottom of the listing sheet can be used to explain other features not already mentioned, such as, paneled playroom, screened-in porch, swimming pool, tennis court, greenhouse, etc.

It is important to list those items that would normally be included in the sale of your house but you plan to take with you. A statement at the bottom could read: "The following item(s) excluded from the purchase price . . ."

When you have completed your listing sheet and have had copies made, you're ready to begin the next step: Presentation.

The way to a successful presentation of your house is advertising. Your classified ad is the major source you have to bring potential buyers to your house.

Most homeowners can probably write a passable ad simply by copying the style in any newspaper's real estate section. By following a few pointers in this chapter, you should be able to create a classified ad that will not only be accurate but *noticeable*.

Begin your ad with an eye-catching headline, one that will stand out from the hundreds of other classified ads that appear every day.

Select the most appealing features of your house and work it into the headline. Remember, you're creating a picture of your house and its special virtues. One word (an adjective, preferably) will have to sum up the feeling your house offers. Combine this descriptive word with the word or phrase that best describes your type of dwelling. Keep in mind the economic group you are trying to reach, and play with descriptive words until you have a phrase that will pique the buyer's interest. Here are some examples:

- Spacious Family Colonial
- Walk to Shopping
- Secluded Forest Setting
- For the Active Family
- Attention Horse Lovers
- Perfect Starter Home
- Formal Rose Gardens
- French Farmhouse
- Well-kept Expandable Cape
- Old World Charm—Brand New Interior
- At the Beach
- Handyman's Dream
- Exclusive-Area Contemporary
- Fish on Private Lake
- Peace and Quiet
- Ideal for Couple
- Move-in Condition
- Traffic-Free Area
- Rolling Hills
- Architect Designed
- Year-Round Swiss Chalet
- All-Brick Colonial
- Fantastic Bargain
- Paved Private Road
- Perfect for Entertaining
- Executive Area
- Room for the Kids
- Guest Cottage on Property

- Priced to Sell
- Change Your Lifestyle
- Three Fireplaces
- Cathedral Ceiling
- Mother-in-law Apartment
- In-Ground Pool

Certain adjectives will provoke predictable responses in buyers. Play to the prospective buyer's needs in your headline. If you have room in your headline, insert an additional phrase, beyond the concise description. Use a phrase that will stimulate the buyer to respond now. For instance: LEAVING AREA, MUST SELL FAST; CALL RIGHT NOW!; REDUCED FOR QUICK SALE.

Always insert the words "By Owner" above your headline. Prospects generally have the feeling they will be getting a better deal by bargaining directly with the owner rather than with a broker.

Your ad should be honest, pointing out the special virtues that distinguish your home. Do not try to compete with the real estate brokers to see who can write the most bombastic ad. They are out to get clients, you are out to sell your house. If you play their game, you will waste time and money by attracting buyers with an unrealistic offer. Your purpose is to attract serious buyers who are willing to pay a fair price for your property. The most important job your ad has to do is to stimulate prospects to get further information about your house.

Give some thought to who your prospective buyers really are. If you live in a neighborhood with a large percentage of young families, don't write an ad that appeals to an audience of retired people. Make sure ads sing with the special features of your house that will grab your prospects. Is your backyard fenced in for children? Are you close enough to a park that would interest the senior citizen? Are there colleges nearby that might be of interest to a young couple? Mention these features and your ad will reach the appropriate family for your neighborhood.

The headline is designed to get your prospect's attention. The body of your ad should inform your buyer of the facts about your house: the location, number of rooms, bedrooms, bathrooms, patios, family room, screened-in porch, etc. (Refer to your listing sheet for a summary of all this information.) Use flattering words and phrases. Describe your *luxurious* master suite, or your *oak-paneled* family room. Tell your buyers about the *cozy* fireplace and the *formal* dining room. Always give a little extra descriptive space to describe your kitchen. Point out the style—a "gourmet's delight," "family style," a "real country kitchen," "large eat-in kitchen," etc. Does it have special features like a self-cleaning oven, hardwood cabinets, separate pantry, bay window?

If you have space in your ad try to avoid the use of abbreviations. Most real estate broker's ads contain abbreviations for every possible part of the house. You've probably seen a broker's ad that reads like this:

> Lvly Contemp 3 Bdrms
> 1½ Bth frml din rm
> Frpl in fam rm 2 cr gar

This may be easy enough for a real estate broker to decode, but the ad is cold and unappealing. You may save some money by limiting the number of ad lines you buy, but you will end up losing readers. Make your ads attractive and simple; avoid being dull and difficult to read.

Mention your asking price prominently (but not in the headline, unless it's an obvious steal), and be firm. Don't ever use the phrase "willing to negotiate" or any other words that imply your price is flexible. If you are having an open house, mention this in bold print either at the top or bottom of your ad. (Be sure to mention to the newspaper that your headline should appear in *bold print.*)

How about a heavy border around your ad to set it apart from the others? It may cost a little more but you just might catch the eye of the buyer you've been waiting for.

Near the end of your ad, put the words "Principals Only." This puts brokers on notice that they should avoid bothering you (and tying up your phone) in an attempt to get you as a client. This also lets prospective buyers feel even more certain that they are dealing directly with the owner.

Your final words should reinforce your reader to take action. End your ad with words that do not leave your prospective buyer hanging: "Call Immediately," "Don't Wait" or "Stop-by Saturday 1–3." And don't forget your phone number.

Write several different versions of your ad before you decide which one to use. If you are going to advertise in more than one newspaper, you might even try a different ad in each paper to see which one works the best.

If you find it difficult to come up with strong advertising copy, many newspapers have people in their classified departments who will be able to offer some suggestions.

Here are some typical ads you may find helpful:

BY OWNER
FAMILY NEIGHBORHOOD—GOOD LOCATION

Rambling contemporary on one-acre wooded lot. 4 bedrooms, 2½ baths with formal dining room. Perfect for entertaining. Family room with stone fireplace, 2-car garage. Many extras including gourmet kitchen. Principals Only. $63,900. Call now 555-3241

BY OWNER
STURDY, EXPANDABLE CAPE

Cozy paneled living room with fireplace, eat-in kitchen, 2 bedrooms, 1½ baths, finished basement, garage, stream on property. Priced for immediate sale at $25,000. Principals Only. Call for appt. 555-6521

BY OWNER
QUALITY LARGE HOME
EASY WALK TO SHOPPING

Gracious colonial in family neighborhood. 4 bedrooms, 2½ baths. Huge country kitchen with wall oven. Screened porch, 2-car garage, income apartment. Will go fast at $68,500. Principals Only. OPEN HOUSE SUN. 2–4 or call for appt. 555-3675

BY OWNER
RUSTIC COTTAGE FOR HANDYMAN

With a little work this rustic beauty can be vacation paradise. 2 bedrooms, 1 bath, knotty pine living room with brick fireplace. Eat-in kitchen with lovely view of private pond. Mature pines on 2 full acres. Principals Only. Call 555-7964. $16,500 Firm.

If there is more than one newspaper in your community or region, determine which paper is going to be read by people most likely to be interested in your property. Which newspaper would appeal to you if you were looking for a house like yours? If there's a paper in your area that has a special section for real estate ads, consider placing your ad there too. The idea is to reach the maximum number of likely buyers in your area.

The Sunday edition of your newspaper probably carries the largest number of real estate ads. Most serious buyers will not miss this edition. It may be wiser to spend your money on a larger ad for Sunday's paper, rather than two or three inserts in the daily paper. A buyer will usually save the Sunday edition even if he cannot call or see a house that day. You may get telephone calls on Wednesday or Thursday from your ad in last Sunday's edition.

If your ad doesn't draw anything but flies after appearing for two consecutive weeks, change it. You may have chosen the wrong newspaper, or the appeal may be wrong, or the newspaper may have gotten your phone number wrong. (Check your ad every day.) If you're inundated with many callers, but few follow through with a visit, your ad may be unrealistic.

How much you spend on your ad can be guided somewhat by the asking price of your house. As a general guide, remove the last three digits of your asking price to arrive at a realistic expenditure. If your asking price is $35,000, $35 for one insertion would be a reasonable expense. At a $75,000 asking price an ad could cost $75 but will probably cost less.

If you want to put a sign in your front yard, don't copy the style of signs used by brokers. Real estate brokers' signs usually list only the name of the agency and the telephone number above the telephone number of the house for sale. In this way a broker can profit from a caller who is not qualified or interested in the house where the sign appears.

Your sign should be directed to the people who may have missed your newspaper ad.

There are ready-made signs that say "For Sale," with a space to write your telephone number. Unless your lettering talent is unusually superior, have a sign painted by a professional. Never display a sign that looks amateur or messy. It will be taken as an indication of your home.

Signs vary in size but standard "For Sale" signs are usually 21″ high by 27″ wide, or 24″ high by 36″ wide. The large sign is more desirable when it is placed far from the street. Dark letters on a white background make the sign readable at night. Prices for signs vary depending on the size; most cost from $15 to $25.

Use "For Sale by Owner" as the heading for your sign so that buyers will know immediately your house is not being offered by a real estate broker. Below the heading indicate "For Appointment Call"—and list both your home phone and your business phone if you are out during the day. Make sure the printing is large enough to be read easily from the street.

Unless you live on a one-way street have both sides of the sign painted. Place the sign in your front yard at right angles to your house. Be sure the sign is not blocked by large trees and bushes or by parked cars.

If you have planned an open house, attach a small "Open" sign to your "For Sale" sign on the day of your open house. Smaller "For Sale" and "Open" signs should be placed at the corner of your street on open house day. This will help lead prospects directly to your house.

Before you buy and erect a sign on your front lawn,

check your zoning regulations. Some communities forbid "For Sale" signs on private property.

An open house on Saturday and Sunday afternoons usually brings streams of visitors on the first weekend your ad appears. Be prepared. It is an invitation to potential buyers to stop by and inspect your home without making an appointment. It is also an invitation to casual Sunday drivers with nothing better to do. It can be annoying to have strangers drop by unannounced, and you can't really screen visitors, but the more people you attract the better chance you will have discovering people who are seriously interested.

Since the purpose of holding an open house is to attract people, the more days you can hold your house open the more likely you are to find prospects. Display your "Open" sign every day you plan to be home.

Give a copy of your listing sheet to all interested buyers. They can then refer to the sheet later as a reminder of your house and its features. With a little luck the sun will shine brightly on the days you have your open house.

In addition to a general open house, consider a private open house for your neighbors. Take them on a tour. (How many of your neighbors have ever seen the upstairs or basement of your home?) Neighbors can be your most active supporters. They might recommend your home to friends or others they know who are in the market for a house. They are obviously sold on living in your neighborhood and it's natural for them to want the kind of people they will be happy with living on their block. Remember to give each of your neighbors a listing sheet they can take away to show or give to likely candidates they may know.

If you can't get your neighbors together for an open

house, put listing sheets, with a short note attached, in their mailboxes. Ask them, as neighbors, to help in the sale of your home. Mention why you are moving, without being offensive. (Don't say you are leaving for a better neighborhood.) Ask them to contact you if they have any questions or want to see the house. You may discover that there's a neighbor who doesn't want to leave the neighborhood but needs a bigger house.

Circulating listing sheets around your area is the least expensive way to inform people that your house is for sale. Displaying your listing sheet at neighborhood stores is another way of reaching a large number of people. Many supermarkets have community bulletin boards that, in essence, give you free advertising space. Large companies sometimes have housing offices for the convenience of employees and will probably welcome your listing sheet. Campus housing departments are another free source of leads. Ask them to put a record of your house on file and to place your listing sheet on the bulletin board.

Church meeting rooms, beauty parlors and drugstores have regular traffic and are also good places to post your listing sheet.

Community agencies that work in conjunction with the Chamber of Commerce, such as Welcome Wagon or New Neighbors, are frequently contacted by families planning to relocate in your area. Call these organizations first, and if you can, drop off several listing sheets at their offices.

Use your listing sheet for quick reference when responding to phone inquiries about your house. All the information your potential buyer will need to know is contained in this sheet. Offer to mail one out to your prospect that day.

You must realize that advertising does not do the

selling job for you. At best, it will take the serious buyer to the point of showing sincere interest in your house. It is then your job as salesman to complete the sale.

It's now time to discuss negotiation.

If your classified ad is working, your first contact with your prospect will probably be by telephone. Be enthusiastic, but not pushy or overanxious. Sound like you're pleased to hear from your caller. When your prospect says that he has seen your ad in the paper, answer on a positive note: Something like, "I'm glad that you've answered the ad." Ask the caller's name right away so you can refer to him or her by name during the conversation. "Would you like me to tell you something about the house?" is a good opening question. Answer all inquiries courteously, without elaborating. Try to arrange an appointment if your caller shows some interest. If he is unable to make an appointment, offer to send your listing sheet. Receiving a listing sheet may spark enough interest for the prospect to call for an appointment later.

Be positive and enthusiastic about the uniqueness of your house. "The house is wonderful. We really hate to leave, but I'm being transferred. I think you'll love it too. It's only a mile from downtown and the kids can walk to school. Is Sunday about two o'clock convenient for you?"

Now you have to get ready to show your house. If you have never been a salesperson, it's a good idea to learn some techniques that professionals use to sell their merchandise. Perhaps because of the sizable amounts of money involved, there seems to be a basic need on the part of the buyer to resist as long as possible. The buyer does not want to feel he is an easy mark.

You have to take prospective buyers' objections seriously while gently persisting that the objections be spelled out specifically. Going over the objections a few times with positive answers will usually cause the frivolous buyer to give up his game. The sincere prospect will listen intently to your arguments, while the game player will eventually abandon them.

Most buyers are attracted to a particular piece of property by other factors than the number of bedrooms and the name of your street. A decision to buy is usually influenced by a number of emotions. Unfortunately for the seller it is difficult to measure or predict these feelings in advance. This section of the chapter will give you suggestions to help you "read" your buyer, then exploit this reading so you can make the quickest sale at the highest possible price.

You can begin to study your prospective buyer's needs as soon as he or she approaches your front door. If he has his family with him, it should be an immediate signal that his family's desires and interests are probably important to him. A prospect who drives up in a flashy car will give you some idea of his need for prestige and appearance.

Do not ask too many questions. Solicit only that information you can use to understand the prospect's needs more thoroughly, such as where he lives and what kind of work he does. (These kinds of questions are not really too personal and the answers are important in helping you sell features of your house.) If your prospect is transferring to a company in town emphasize the location of your house and its accessibility to his office.

Try to limit your questions to those that your prospect will respond to positively. "Don't you think the garden is lovely?" is much better than, "Are you a gardener?" "Don't you think the playroom is a perfect spot for a pool table?" is much better than, "Do you play pool?"

Asking well-phrased questions will let your prospect feel you are really interested in him and his opinions. He will also be more likely to respond to you and your opinions. Drawing out your prospects with the right questions will eventually bring his needs to the surface.

Overtalking and overselling are major problems for the inexperienced salesperson. By asking tactful questions you are allowing your prospective buyer to speak and you avoid hogging the conversation. Asking questions that call for positive answers avoids the likelihood of getting into arguments with your buyer. Arguments cause tension and are distracting. A professional salesman's credo says if you win the argument you are bound to lose the sale.

Try to be more concerned with the prospect's needs than your own. Don't try to oversell your house by talking about how it satisfied *your* needs. The buyer is concerned only with how it will satisfy him. Above all, don't be negative. Any objections your buyer raises should be analyzed silently by you: Are they real objections or does the buyer just feel he has to be negative about something or he'll lose the advantage?

If his objections seem to be directed at your taste in home furnishings, he is probably just a "looker." When he begins to doubt whether there are enough closets for his family, take him seriously.

There are several ways to overcome objections with an affirmative response. If there is a real deficiency, agree that "Yes, there are not enough closets in the bedrooms, but there is plenty of storage space in the attic. We store our out-of-season clothing there, and we have enough room downstairs for everything else."

Changing the subject entirely will often help. If the deficiency is obvious and unsolvable, just agree quietly and go on to something else. Never lie outright, you may be creating a reason for the buyer to mistrust you about everything else.

Try to overcome some objections by pointing to other better qualities of your house. If you do not have a guest room and it seems to be a major drawback for your prospect, tell him that you have always used the family room for guests and since it has its own bathroom you have never felt unnecessarily burdened with overnight guests.

Always listen carefully to flaws your buyer mentions. Not only will you be able to assess his needs better, but you can frequently use these objections to point out how his needs can be met another way.

Showing the less favorable parts of your house first may head off objections later. The buyer may be so entranced with the more attractive features he may even forget that there is no fireplace in the family room. You must be knowledgeable and realistic about your home's shortcomings so that you aren't caught off guard when your prospect notices a particular deficiency.

Remember that most people who look for a house think of their search as an exciting adventure. It is an exhilarating experience for a family to "move up" and you must be willing to share this experience with them by nourishing their excitement with your enthusiasm.

Once you have prepared yourself to deal with your house's drawbacks, you must be ready to replace objections with positive features. One way is to stress your house's hidden values. These are the features of the house that cannot readily be seen but contribute to its quality and comfort. It may be a construction technique, like a 12″-thick foundation or a built-in humidifying system. Whatever it might be it should be pointed out as strongly as the more obvious features of your house. Explaining these unseen features may spell the difference in the prospect's choice of your house over another. Basically, though, it will be the cumulative effect of many desirable features that contribute to the prospect's ultimate decision to buy a house, and the more he knows about your house the more ammunition he has to decide in your favor.

When you're talking to a prospect, use his language. Put in layman's terms the features the buyer may be unfamiliar with. Don't display deep technical knowledge that may confuse or intimidate your buyer (or, worst of all, make him feel stupid). It may be beneficial to have a service man come to your house to explain certain things that you do not fully understand. It's vital that you be confident of your responses in advance.

You should also carefully preplan your house tour. Never allow your prospect to wander through the house unguided. Rehearse a number of tours to satisfy different types of buyers you are likely to encounter. Begin each tour on a positive note and end on a positive note. Be ready to open all the closets and to inspect the basement and attic. Choose a comfortable place to sit with your prospect after the initial tour. Maybe in front of the fireplace in the family room, or in your beautiful remodeled kitchen. Be sure you pick an attractive spot to sit and talk. Your buyer will definitely notice the surroundings.

Know about and be ready to discuss all your appliances. Have unexpired warranties on hand to show the prospect. Be enthusiastic about the quality of the items you have bought for your house. Have the asking prices ready for any appliances or other things you want to sell separately. But don't try to sell everything at once. Wait until you're asked the price.

Have a map of the local area on hand to show where your house is in relation to schools, shopping and transportation. The fact that the bus to the downtown area stops on your corner may be a major factor in your sale if someone in the family has to use public transportation. If your house is within walking distance of the local "Y" it may be important to children in the prospect's family.

If you haven't already, find out details about local and private schools, as well as other community facilities that may be of interest to a buyer, such as commuting schedules on the local train, town activities, fire and police service, etc.

One last thought before you greet your first prospect. Try to look successful. Since you are a temporary spokesman for your neighborhood, it's helpful (and flattering to your prospect) to appear neat and mildly prosperous. It's not necessary to wear formal clothes, but avoid the possibility of offending. Paint-spattered, torn work clothes may make some prospects feel uncomfortable about you. You want the prospect to feel positive about you, and consequently, positive about the house. If it means dressing early on Sunday morning, play the part. It just may make the difference.

One point on etiquette. An inspection tour is not a social visit. There is no need for you to serve refreshments. Don't try to prolong the visit in the hopes that your hospitality will stimulate a sale. Your interests are better served if you and your prospects have a polite, courteous but strictly businesslike relationship. It is far less difficult to bargain and negotiate with a stranger than with a new friend.

Here are a few last-minute touches to keep in mind. They will help make your house as inviting as possible to your visitors. The house should be clean and airy and above all, cheerful. If you are showing your house during the day (and you should avoid nighttime appointments, if possible) pull back the drapes and let in as much sunlight as possible. The sunshine will be cheery and will help brighten furniture that may be worn and old. If you must see prospects in the evening, remember to leave the porch light on and any outdoor garden lighting you have.

Don't cook right before your prospects arrive, especially if the gourmet treat you're making will produce strong odors. The only cooking aromas should be the warm smells of fresh baking bread, or a fresh pot of coffee. While the house should be thoroughly aired out, be sure it's not too cold in the winter or too hot in the summer.

Pets can annoy prospects. Their odors may be offensive and some prospects may even be allergic to animals. Keep pets outside if possible.

Try to keep the house as quiet as possible. The television should be turned off and the children should be asked to play quietly (at a friend's house, if possible). Distractions may prevent your visitors from forming a valid opinion of the house itself. If you live near unavoidable noise, such as highway traffic, show your house when the noise is at its lightest. Midday is the best time.

Every room in the house should be neat and clean— the beds made, clothes put away, dishes washed and put away. If you do not have the time to spend cleaning your house every day, it may be worth an investment of $20 a week to have a cleaning service do all the heavy work for you. The investment is minimal when you think of the money it could mean from a quick sale of your house. A neat and orderly presentation is not only more attractive it helps stimulate a prospect's mood to buy.

Always greet your prospect at the front door. It is confusing to a new visitor to be ushered in through a side door, even if your family uses that door all the time. It will make it less difficult for the prospect to assess your floor plan from the right perspective. Your front door is usually the most dramatic approach to your house, and your prospect will remember with keen awareness his first impression of your house. (He may be thinking about how his mother-in-law will feel about your house, or how impressed his friends will be as they walk through *his* house.)

You should now be ready to greet your first prospect and lead a charming tour of your home. Hopefully, at the end of the tour your prospect will make a statement such as, "Maybe I should consider it," "I think my wife and I should talk it over," or "I'll have to bring my parents before we decide." These kinds of semi-affirmative statements usually mean you've reached a point where you should stop selling and begin closing the deal. Too much more selling will put your buyer off. Once your prospect lets you know that he is seriously considering your house, your job becomes not one of selling but of closing the deal.

Be sure every likely prospect leaves your first meeting with a listing sheet so he can go home and easily recall those special features that may finally convince him to buy.

LISTING SHEET

(PHOTOGRAPH OF YOUR HOUSE)

FOR SALE BY OWNER	OWNER John Anderson RES. PHONE 555-2394 BUS. PHONE 555-6473	Secluded wooded lot Completely modern kitchen on 3-acre parklike setting

350 Worth Street ADDRESS	Bedford COMMUNITY	7 ROOMS	4 BDRMS.	2½ BTH.	$56,900 PRICE

STYLE	Dutch colonial	PATIO	Brick
CONSTRUCTION	Cedar siding	FIREPLACE	Liv. Rm.
AGE	3 yrs.	CARPETS	3 yrs. old
LOT SIZE	3 acres	DRAPES	Dining Rm.
SQ. FT.	2,700	HEAT	Oil—Hot water
LIVING RM.	23 x 12	AIR COND.	Central
DINING RM.	14 x 9	DISHWASHER	Kitchenaid 3 yrs.
FAMILY RM.		DISPOSAL	
BEDROOM 1	18 x 16 Master	STOVE	Sears—self-clean
BEDROOM 2	17 x 15	CITY WATER	Yes
BEDROOM 3	15 x 11	SEWER	Yes
BEDROOM 4	9 x 12	PROPERTY TAX	$1,200
KITCHEN	13 x 12	SCHOOL: ELEM.	Kings Hwy.
BREAKFST. RM.	14 x 9	J.H.S.	Bedford
BASEMENT	Laundry fac.	H.S.	Staples
GARAGE	2 car det.		
CLOSETS	8, 1 walk-in		
		Screened-in porch	
		Circular Driveway	

LISTING SHEET

OWNER

RES. PHONE

FOR SALE
BY OWNER

BUS. PHONE

ADDRESS | COMMUNITY | ROOMS | BDRMS. | BTH. | PRICE |

STYLE	PATIO
CONSTRUCTION	FIREPLACE
AGE	CARPETS
LOT SIZE	DRAPES
SQ. FT.	HEAT
LIVING RM.	AIR COND.
DINING RM.	DISHWASHER
FAMILY RM.	DISPOSAL
BEDROOM 1	STOVE
BEDROOM 2	CITY WATER
BEDROOM 3	SEWER
BEDROOM 4	PROPERTY TAX
KITCHEN	SCHOOL: ELEM.
BREAKFST. RM.	J.H.S.
BASEMENT	H.S.
GARAGE	
CLOSETS	

CHAPTER
4
How to Complete the Sale of Your House

It's unlikely your prospect will make just one tour of your house, and then immediately sign a contract. He will probably need at least two or three trips, probably with additional members of his family and possibly friends.

When your house fits the buyer's needs, and his objections and questions have been answered satisfactorily, closing the sale might seem to be almost automatic. It isn't. Buying a house for many thousands of dollars is a decision no one takes lightly. Don't pressure your prospect at this point. It's difficult enough to retain all the information and selling points that have been made during the days of discussion. Don't risk killing a sale at the last moment by suddenly turning on the pressure.

Resist the temptation to hurry the deal with hard-sell techniques. It may antagonize a prospect and even turn him away from your house. Arguing about some minor point is another good way to lose the sale. Accept graciously unfavorable comments, especially in the area of personal taste. Remember, this is probably the most important financial decision your buyer will ever make. It is normal, even wise, for him to take his time and exercise extreme caution.

It is unlikely that after touring your house, the buyer will come right out and say, "I'd like to buy your house for your asking price." He will probably begin by trying to find out how flexible you are about the price. "Are you willing to take $2,000 less than the asking price?" or "What's your bottom price?" There is only one way you can handle these questions, and that is to sit down and discuss them. Don't get insulted or answer in monosyllables.

If you were using a real estate broker, the broker would insist on a written proposal from the buyer at this point to prove his sincerity, even if the offer was extremely low. A broker works on the basis that a seller just might accept a ridiculously low price and then a binding contract can be formed. It is, of course, to the broker's interests to sell the property even at a "lowball" price. But as the salesperson of your own house, it's to your advantage to keep the negotiations at the level of a polite, informal discussion.

Remember, too, that if you accept your buyer's first low offer and he subsequently decides to withdraw from the sale (after a formal contract has been drawn) your only alternative will be to hire an attorney and take the buyer to court—an expensive and time-wasting proposition. It is unlikely that a buyer will even begin to negotiate with you if he is not sincerely interested in purchasing your property. Once you do agree to terms you can then proceed with the written forms.

Negotiation is the time when the buyer and the seller are going to be presenting their individual viewpoints. Each will try to convince the other that his or her own position is the more sound. Remember, here, that you are trying to convince the buyer that your position is reasonable. You should not be trying to overpower him.

It is the buyer who should begin the negotiations. He already knows your asking price. (It's listed on your fact sheet.) It is up to him to suggest a lower figure. If *you* begin and happen to suggest a figure $1,000 lower than your asking price, you'll never know if your buyer would have been willing to settle for $500 instead of $1,000 less, or even if the buyer would have paid your full asking price. An appropriate response to a buyer's inquiry about price is to turn it around and ask him what he is willing to pay.

For the sake of this discussion, let's say the asking price of your house is $42,500. You have asked the buyer how much he is willing to pay and he says he can probably come up with $41,500. Your next step is to ask him to put it in writing. If he agrees to a written statement you know that he is seriously interested in purchasing your house, and that he is willing to spend at least $41,500. If he will not agree to put it in writing, he is probably not really ready to pay even that much. Your next step will be to encourage your buyer to raise his price, or at least make some commitment for your consideration.

Now is the time to call on all your powers of perception and empathy. Encourage the buyer to keep talking. Concentrate on what the buyer is saying about your property and you should be able to determine not only how he actually feels about your house but any information he may be holding back. A wife or husband who constantly tell each other to keep quiet is a tip that one of them is *really* interested in your property and might be willing to pay more than they initially offered. Your buyer does not want to appear over-enthusiastic. He is also trying to get the best deal possible. He wants to keep his bargaining position open. Make sure you never interrupt your buyer at this point. Concentrate your energy on picking up clues to the buyer's real intentions.

Even if you violently disagree with the buyer's viewpoint, let him finish what he is saying before you respond. If you fail to listen carefully you may not understand the reasoning he is using and you may end up shouting and arguing. Fights between sellers and prospects always lead to a dead end. Try to understand his feelings. You will not accomplish anything by making debating points.

The prospect's arguments may be valid, in which case the best you can do is agree with him and hope you can turn the objections around with a positive response. For example, if the buyer says, "The train station is only a block from your house" you cannot argue that point. But if the prospect says that the noise is probably intolerable, you may say that you also thought it would be a problem when you bought the house, but after a few days you hardly noticed it at all.

If you really disagree on some point, try to support your position with facts—politely. By saying, "I understand what you're saying, but I have to disagree," you are letting the buyer know you're on his side. Let your buyer think that you have confidence in his decisions. He will, in turn, rely on your judgment.

Unless you are clearly at the end of negotiations, try to maintain your bargaining position as long as possible. If your buyer states flatly that he will not go any higher than $41,500, imply that you cannot accept $41,500, but that you might consider $42,000. The buyer may then reject this offer but you still have your option to reduce the price to $41,750 or $41,600 or even $41,500!

There may come a point in the negotiations where neither the buyer nor you are willing to bargain further. You have given your final price and the buyer refuses to go any higher to meet it. It is essential at this point to suggest taking a break. It might be a good idea to let the buyers talk privately for a while. It will also give you an opportunity to discuss your position with your family. This break may release the tension that is bound to build up when making a financial decision of this kind. If, after a short break, you still can't resolve your differences, it might be a good idea to part and suggest you all get together at a later date.

Get in touch with the buyer the next day and perhaps offer to reduce your asking price by $250 or so. Your buyer may respond to your desire to compromise and go up $250, or $500. The $250 or $500 is a small sum when you consider it as a percentage of the cost of the house.

Try to be as reasonable as possible about the small things. If the discussion with the buyer centers around whether or not you are willing to leave the wall-to-wall carpet in the bedroom, it's to your advantage to throw it in. After you have waited for a buyer for a time, a few hundred dollars' worth of carpet should not lose the sale for you.

If you find that months go by and you have not received any offers, or you are inundated with offers that are far below your asking price, you have probably estimated the market value of your house unrealistically. In either case, it is time to reassess your property and consider changing your asking price.

Once you and the buyer have reached a satisfactory conclusion to your negotiations, you must now insist on a written statement of your buyer's offer.

The Binder

There is a time between the verbal agreement on terms and the signing of a formal contract when you and the buyer should be held together, informally but *in writing.* It will usually take the form of a receipt and binder signed in duplicate. The receipt is for the buyer's deposit (usually a token $50 to $250) and the binder states that the buyer officially agreed to make this initial offer. It is to the buyer's advantage to sign the binder so that you'll take the house off the market for a time, and it's to your advantage to get the buyer's consent in writing to the price and terms until a more formal sales contract can be drawn up by your attorney.

Remember, though, the binder is an agreement between the buyer and seller to enter a more formal contract. If your and the prospect's lawyers cannot get you both to agree on the detailed terms of the more formal sales contract (or one of you decides for some reason not to go to contract) what was once a preliminary agreement can become a legally binding document. This is where the court fights may begin.

The binder includes the date, description of the property, purchase price, total down payment required, whatever financial arrangements are to be made and the conditions of the sale. A sample binder will be found at the end of this chapter.

Here is a description of binder information, and its legal ramifications. (It is still advisable to deal with your real estate attorney when assembling the information to be included on your binder.)

Description of the Property

This ordinarily requires only the street number and town where the property is located. If there's any chance for confusion (say your house is on a piece of subdivided property), use a more elaborate description. For instance; "Three-story frame dwelling located at 47 Bryer Lane in the town of Lancaster, state of Missouri."

Financing

This is a complex step in the selling of your home. An entire detailed section on financing will be found in Chapter 5. For the purpose of the binder it's important that the terms of the sale be set forth. In the rare event it is to be an all-cash sale, then a simple statement such as "This is to be an all-cash sale" is clear enough. If, as is likely, your buyer must obtain a mortgage, he will want a clause that will release him from his obligation if he can't get financing.

Before you get to the point where you decide what financing arrangements will be included in the binder, try to be sure your buyer can come up with the money. You can get some idea of the financial status of your buyer by the kind of job he has, the kind of home he lives in now, even the kind of clothes he's wearing and the car he owns. Of course you cannot come right out and ask him what his income is but you should get an indication of his financial ability during your negotiations and discussions.

If it seems your buyer will have a problem with finances, there are a number of ways you can offer to help ease the burden, depending of course on your own financial position. We discuss each alternative here and how it should be spelled out in the binder.

Assuming your existing loan. In this case it is imperative that you both be aware of what the current outstanding balance is of your mortgage. The buyer will also want to know what his costs will be to assume the loan, what the monthly payments are, including the interest rate and taxes. Speak to an officer of your lending institution beforehand to determine this information accurately, as well as other alternatives your buyer might have in obtaining financing. This clause in the binder should also state that the buyer will be excused from the sale if the conditions upon which this loan is assumed are misrepresented in any way. The financing clause, in this case, would read:

> "The buyer will assume the existing loan with (*name of financial institution*), the approximate amount being (*the amount of your unpaid mortgage balance*), monthly payments being $_____, including the interest at _____% per year. Buyer is also required to pay the lender $_____ for assuming this loan. The purchase of this property is conditional upon the status of the loan being as represented."

New Loan. If the buyer is going to get a new loan either with your lender or with his own, the sale will be contingent on his getting such financing. Most important here, for the buyer's safety, is a clause that stipulates that the seller is to pay off his loans prior to the transfer of title. This part of the binder should also allow for flexibility on your part, if the buyer cannot get as much financing as he thought he could. The clause, in this case, would read as follows:

> "The buyer will obtain a loan from (*name of financial institution*) in the amount of $_____.
> If the loan is less than the maximum amount set forth as $_____, the down payment will increase accordingly, the purchase price to remain

the same. The seller agrees to pay off all prior loans of record before transfer of title. This offer is subject to and contingent upon the buyer's ability to obtain said loan."

Obtaining a second mortgage. A second mortgage can be obtained by a buyer in the event that a lending institution won't give him enough money to cover the mortgage. You, as the seller, may be in a position to offer the extra money to your buyer as a second mortgage, or another lending institution may be willing to offer the second mortgage. If you do decide to give the buyer a second mortgage, your real estate attorney should handle the written loan agreement, the payment schedule and your legal protection. A second mortgage could amount to thousands of dollars and you must be able to cover yourself legally in the event that the buyer defaults on his payments. *Do not offer second mortgage help without the advice of your attorney.*

A second mortgage clause in the binder would read:

"The seller has agreed to a second mortgage in the amount of $_____, the difference between the purchase price and the total amount of the first loan plus the down payment. The note is to be paid back at $_____ per month with interest at the rate of _____% per year. This note is payable _____ years from the date of this transaction."

If you are giving your buyer a second mortgage, your attorney will probably advise you to include a clause that requires the buyer to pay back your note before he may resell the property.

Physical Condition of the Property

Most home buyers will insist on a building inspection before they "go to contract." They will usually employ professional inspectors to assess the physical condition of the property. Inspectors then offer a written evaluation of their findings. The "Physical Condition" part of the binder should include a clause that stipulates that the property undergo inspection approval before the buyer obligates himself to the purchase. You should give the buyer seven days to have his inspection completed. If, after seven days the buyer does not indicate his *disapproval*, he is then responsible for the purchase agreement. This clause may also include inspection by a pest-control expert. Your buyer will undoubtedly want to have the house inspected for termites. This should be done at the buyer's expense on the condition that if the inspection shows any signs of termite infestation, you will agree to rid the premises of such pests or the buyer can cancel his agreement.

The clause can read as follows:

"The buyer will have the property inspected at his own expense in relation to the physical structure and pest infestation. The report and its approval by the buyer will be completed no later than seven days from the date of this transaction. If after the seven-day period the buyer has not informed the seller of his disapproval of said reports, the seller will deem the buyer responsible for the purchase of said property."

It is your legal obligation as seller to maintain your property in its current condition until the formal sales contract is signed. Your buyer may insist that a clause be inserted in the binder giving him that assurance. The buyer cannot back out of the deal if you do not maintain the property unless it is so stipulated in the binder. But he may decide to sue if the property is noticeably damaged. This clause is likely to include such items as all appliances that are to be left as part of the property, electrical system, heating mechanisms, etc.

Other Miscellaneous Items

It is your obligation to list in the binder those items you have decided to take with you if they are normally considered part of the property. If these things are not specifically itemized, the buyer may sue you for misrepresentation and recover all items he feels are part of the property. You can protect yourself with the insertion of this kind of clause:

"The purchase price does not include the following items that are affixed to said property: wall-to-wall carpeting in master bedroom, dining room fixture, interior shutters in family room. The buyer does agree to purchase the following personal property found at said premises: refrigerator, washer and drier, the total purchase price being $_____."

If you agreed to perform certain tasks before the transfer of title they should be spelled out in the binder, again stipulating that the sale is contingent on certain items being repaired, refurbished, etc.

Your buyer's attorney may also want to add a clause about the sale of your buyer's present home, especially if that money is needed to purchase your home. If there is no clause to this effect, the buyer will be in breach of his commitment if he fails to buy your house, regardless of the sale of his own home. He will then have to forfeit his deposit.

Once you and the buyer have negotiated the above points satisfactorily, you *both* sign the binder. Now it is virtually impossible to back out of the deal, unless the conditions of the binder are not met.

A blank binder will be found at the end of this chapter.

The Lawyer

Now you have found someone willing to purchase your property and that buyer has assumed the legal responsibility for the purchase with a signed binder and deposit. You have agreed with your buyer on the terms and the price, but there are still some details to be finalized before you can actually "go to contract." Title evidence, deeds, defaults, risk of loss, implied agreements and other legal arrangements must still be worked out. Unless you are a practicing attorney there is no way you can handle these problems yourself. If you've held off until now, don't wait any longer, hire a real estate attorney to represent you.

Your lawyer's job is to protect your bargain, record it and then bring together all legal aspects of the sale for a final closing contract. He is the most qualified to put together a practical and legally binding contract agreement between you and your buyer.

The following steps will help you in selecting the best attorney for your contract work and later, the final closing.

Choose a lawyer experienced in residential sales. Real estate law varies greatly from state to state. Each state makes its own laws regarding real estate in that state. Also, each community within that state has its own local regulations that are frequently laws of tradition relating to that particular area. Because legal practices can vary from community to community, you should hire a lawyer who is familiar with your community's local law.

If you used a local lawyer when you bought your house and were satisfied with his services, give him a call. He probably has copies of your deed, title and other documents you will need for your contract and closing. If you don't know a local real estate lawyer, ask neighbors or friends to recommend one. Your bank or loan association can also refer you to a lawyer. Ask an officer at the institution that holds your mortgage what the fee usually is for an attorney who works on houses in your price range. This will at least give you some guidelines when you find a satisfactory lawyer.

Tell your lawyer, at your first meeting, that you are selling your house without the assistance of a broker. He then will understand that he will be required to bring together certain documents a broker would normally locate and collect. And before you go any further ask him what his fee will be to complete the entire transaction. Many sellers are hit with surprising legal bills at the closing because their lawyers did not give them an itemized listing of fees for all legal matters pertaining to the sale. You must also tell your lawyer of any potential complications, such as a second mortgage to the buyer, plans to sell with F.H.A. financing, a recent divorce that could affect the money you receive from the sale. The first conference is the time to bring out anything that would require additional documents for your final contract. Make sure you know at the outset if the lawyer is going to charge extra for this additional paper work. You want to avoid being shocked if he adds them to his fee at the time of closing (when it's too late to change lawyers).

After you've found an attorney to your liking, the biggest part of your job is completed. Except for gathering documents, your attorney should handle the remaining arrangements. Keep aware of what your lawyer is doing and read all documents pertaining to the sale thoroughly, especially those that stipulate dollar amounts.

Lawyers usually have a practice of fixing a standard fee of 1 percent of the selling price of a house to handle contract and closing, but this practice is changing. If the first attorney you visit quotes a standard fee, or a high fee (because you don't have a real estate broker), then by all means *shop around*. There's nothing wrong with negotiating a fee with a lawyer.

In any event, do everything possible to get your lawyer to itemize all his fees *in writing*. If the lawyer is amenable, offer to help him by collecting documents from City Hall, the bank, tax assessor's office, etc., so that his time (and fee) can be reserved for more sophisticated legal work.

The Title Search

The only real problem you may run into at this point is the title search. When your buyer purchases your property he assumes he is buying the three-bedroom house he inspected. That is not always necessarily true. Possession by itself is not legal evidence of ownership. The only acceptable evidence is the public record of ownership. These public records are usually found in the county recorder's office. The only way a buyer can legally assure himself that he is buying what he has seen is to read the title report. This report will include not only the name of the present owner, but evidence of any other interests in the property. Although it's not likely, the buyer doesn't know whether you are only renting the property, or maybe there's a lien against the property. The buyer must protect himself from all unknown encumbrances upon the property. Your deed itself is not evidence enough of total ownership.

Title companies are usually hired to do the title search for the buyer. The buyer's lawyer will instruct him to make the purchase of your house contingent on a title search. Not only will the title search reveal other possible claims on your property, it will also show such possible restrictions as zoning variances against building additions to the property or whether sewer lines will interfere with the swimming pool he hopes to build.

The buyer's attorney will also instruct his client to protect himself with a policy from a title insurance company. The title insurance company insures the buyer against any future encumbrances against the property after he buys it. The title insurance company will research all titles of record and then guarantee the buyer that the information it uncovers is a true representation of the facts. If there is a discrepancy, it is the title insurance company who is responsible for assuming the risk of damages.

Since the regulations regarding title insurance vary from state to state, check the practice in your community with your attorney. (Southern California, for instance, requires the buyer to purchase his own title insurance, while northern California requires the seller to purchase title insurance for the buyer.) The cost of title insurance ranges between $300 and $500 for the average home.

The Sales Contract

Let's assume that all the conditions of the binder have been met. Your buyer has received approval of his title search, the inspection of the property has been completed satisfactorily and the financing has been arranged by the buyer. The binder is signed and you are now ready to begin the next-to-last phase of the sale of your home—the sales contract.

This contract is the formal agreement between the buyer and seller to the terms of sale. There are several areas of agreement that are normally covered in the sales contract.

Signatures of the buyer and seller. All parties involved in the sale must sign the sales contract. If you share ownership of your house both you and your spouse (or co-owner) must sign the contract. If your state has community property laws, your spouse must sign, even though ownership may be in just one name. Have *both* your buyers (assuming they are married) sign the sales agreement. If any legal action against the buyers becomes necessary, you will have both signatures.

Description of the property. The physical description of your property in the binder is not detailed enough for the sales contract. This description is a vital part of the contract. Failure on your part to deliver every item in this description can let your buyer back out of the agreement or sue you by stating that you misrepresented the property.

The description can take many forms. Be sure your lawyer has *all* the information he needs to describe your property. The lawyer should have covered this with you earlier, but if he hasn't here's what you need: the survey description in the title policy, the title policy itself and/or the deed to the property that you received when you bought the house. Do not include any dimensions other than those used on your survey. Any boundaries that are indicated in the description by trees and fences should represent the actual boundaries found in the title policy and not just what you've always assumed them to be. Even being off by one foot could give your buyer grounds for claiming misrepresentation.

All conditions of the property should be as stated in the contract. If you agreed to repair any items, it is your legal obligation at this point to make sure the repairs will be made. All personal property that you are selling with the house must be included with specific prices in the sales contract. Any items that are affixed to the property that you will be taking with you must be listed specifically. By this time there should be no argument about what goes and what remains.

All unexpired warranties for new appliances should be listed in the contract.

The parties' agreement to buy and sell. This is usually just a simple statement that the seller agrees to sell under the conditions of the contract and the buyer agrees to buy under those same conditions.

The financial terms of the sale. This will include the agreed-upon purchase price and the amount of "earnest money" your buyer and you have agreed upon. "Earnest money" is a type of deposit given by the buyer to insure that you are taking your house off the market. Normally, this will be 10 percent of the purchase price. In some cases where the buyer is in need of his cash you may decide to accept as little as half of the 10 percent as earnest money. Most states require that your lawyer hold such funds in a special escrow account.

If your buyer has not received his mortgage approval before the signing of the sales contract, his attorney will insist that a mortgage contingency clause be inserted in the sales contract (even if the clause is already in the binder agreement). If for any reason the buyer's loan is not approved, you will have to refund the entire earnest money payment to the buyer. In most cases a time limit is put on this clause so that you will not have to keep your house off the market for an indefinite period of time. Seven days is usually sufficient time for a loan to be approved, unless you are dealing with F.H.A. or V.A. loans. (These types of mortgage loans will be described in the next chapter.)

If your buyer is waiting to sell his house before he can purchase yours, his attorney may also ask for a "subject to sale" contingency. In this case the clause will usually set aside at least a 60-day period for the buyer to sell his house. This is a painfully long time for you to keep your house off the market. An alternative is for you to accept this subject-to-sale contingency on the condition that you be allowed to keep your house on the market. If another buyer becomes interested, your first buyer has the option to remove the subject-to-sale clause from the contract within 48 hours. If he chooses not to cancel the clause, you will then have the right to dissolve the present contract and proceed with your new buyer.

Evidence of title and deed and other transfer documents. Your buyer's attorney will want to look at your title and deed to be sure they are in "marketable condition" before he will allow his client to proceed with the sale.

Other transfer documents may include a surveyor's map and bills of sale that are to pass between seller and buyer. Bills of sale will be needed for all furnishings and fixtures that you have sold to the buyer for money above the basic purchase price. Evidence will also be needed if you are leaving any unused fuel in your heating fuel tank for the buyer. This amount will be determined at the closing.

Determination of the closing date. The date of the closing is the day that your buyer will actually take possession of your property. Choose your closing date to suit your needs, not the buyer's. If you need the funds from the sale of your present house to purchase your new house, don't let the buyer delay the closing longer than necessary.

In some cases you may find that you will have a gap between the time you close on your old house and close on your new house. This happens frequently. See your banker about a "swing" loan, a temporary loan that will cover you until you close on your new house.

Special agreements between buyer and seller. Because each house sale always has a few unique conditions connected to it, there are special agreements that may have to be made between you and the buyer. If an accident or death occurs between the time of the sales contract and the closing, provisions must be made to serve the best interests of both you and the buyer. Sometimes there are certain zoning regulations that must be carried out, such as occupancy affidavits. These are the kinds of individual problems that should be solved with the help of your attorney.

Sales contract meetings take place either in your attorney's office or the office of your buyer's attorney. Occasionally, if it is inconvenient for all the parties to the sale to meet at a specified time, documents can be signed and given to the respective lawyers who then carry out the sales contract meetings on their own.

The Closing

You have now arrived at the moment when your buyer will take possession of your deed and property and you will take possession of his money. Your responsibilities are at an end. The buyer will now assume complete responsibility for the property.

A formal closing will take place either in the bank where your buyer has received his mortgage loan or at the office of either of your attorneys.

If the closing is to take place at the bank, all financial papers will be prepared and readied by bank personnel. The buyer's attorney will notify the bank of the closing date. The bank will have the certificate of title or mortgage deed, release from the mortgage (if the seller is carrying the existing mortgage) and the warranty note. These papers will be passed to the buyer.

If the closing takes place in a lawyer's office, he will notify the bank of the closing date and the bank will mail all the necessary papers to the attorney's office.

The same procedure will take place there; the buyer receives his deed and the seller receives his money.

There has been much public discussion lately over the high costs of closings. Since real estate transactions tend to be complex, closings, too, are complicated matters. There are going to be costs that are unavoidable.

Your city, county or state levies a tax on every transfer of real estate within its boundaries. Transfer taxes as large as 1 percent of the purchase price are not uncommon.

If there is a new F.H.A. or V.A. loan, you may have to pay for the discount to bring the rates of interest up to market levels. These "points," as they are referred to, are calculated on the interest rate of the new loan and the current market interest-rate for non-insured loans. One point is equal to 1 percent of the amount of the mortgage.

Here are some other closing cost fees that you may encounter: Your attorney's fee; title search fee (paid by either the buyer or the seller depending on local regulations); additional fees to your attorney, such as those for preparation of special documents; all credit reports you may have used to determine your buyer's financial position.

Have your lawyer prepare a closing statement for you *before* the closing date so that all costs can be listed specifically and any questions about charges to you can be answered before the actual closing meeting.

After the signing of all the papers and the passing of checks, all you have to do is turn over your house keys to the buyer. As a courtesy, you can supply him with any information that might make his new home more enjoyable, such as operating instructions for appliances, a list of babysitters or the name of the local newspaper boy.

(Location and date on which binder is signed)   , 19—
received from   *(buyer's full name)*
the sum of $ *(earnest money or deposit)*   as a deposit on
the purchase of the property known as   *(street address
of the house)*   . The total purchase price is $_____.
Total down payment, including the above deposit is
$_____.

_____

_____

(These blank spaces are for all the

various conditions and terms that apply

to your particular transaction.)

_____

_____

_____

_____

This offer shall be irrevocable for a period of _____ days
from the date of this transaction. If parties agree to terms
and conditions of this binder, the buyer will be given possession as of _____, 19___.

CHAPTER
5
Financing

It is, of course, usually up to the buyer to obtain his own mortgage. But home-loan market conditions can change your prospective sale into a lost sale, especially if the mortgage market is tight and your buyer can't qualify for a loan. Be aware of loan conditions in your community when you sell. These conditions could determine not only the pricing of your house, but which buyers will be likely to qualify for a loan.

If you are dealing in a strong home-loan market, it will help your sale. During times of these conditions many lending institutions will authorize loans of up to 80 percent of the value of your house.

In a weak, or tight, loan market, lending institutions usually lower their available percentage to about 75 percent, requiring your buyer to invest more of his own cash. The same buyer who may have qualified for a loan with 80 percent financing may not have enough "down payment cash" to qualify at 75 percent.

Again in a weak loan market there will probably be fewer buyers looking for homes and you may be forced to sell at a lower price.

If the market is strong, you can probably hold out

a little longer and bargain harder, but if the market is weak you can help yourself by being helpful to the prospective buyers.

Now, let's assume you want to dispose of your home and you've found an interested buyer. Before you take your house off the market, and while your buyer finds out if he is qualified for a loan, get some basic information from your buyer on his financial situation.

One way to figure out how much of a mortgage your local lending institutions will give on your house is simply to call and ask. Phone a few home lenders such as banks or savings-and-loan associations. Ask a loan officer if conventional home loans are available in your area. Check their terms. Your personal banker will probably be the one most willing to give you information about your house. Ask for additional referrals if his bank is not making loans at the present time.

Here is what you should find out: the maximum amount of the loan the bank will make, the interest rate and the number of years in which the loan is to be repaid. They will also be able to figure out the monthly principal and interest your buyer will have to pay. At the end of this chapter you will find three mortgage charts which you can fill out with the information you receive from the bank. In the space marked "selling price," fill in the amount you expect to get for your house. On each additional chart fill in, under "down payment," payments of 50 percent, 25 percent and 15 percent. By subtracting the down payment on each chart from the selling price, you can determine the amount of the loan necessary for each different down payment. When you speak to the bank officer, enter the interest rates and terms in the spaces provided. You may also be quoted "points"—the additional fee charged to process the note. The monthly principal payment and interest can be determined from the loan amortization charts found at the end of this chapter.

You can now use your chart to determine, with your buyer, his actual cash needs in each situation.

It is difficult to ask the buyer about his personal finances. Some buyers may come right out and tell you exactly how much cash they have, but more often than not, people are reluctant to give out that kind of information. To help your prospect determine his own qualifications, ask him to fill out a mortgage qualification guide. A blank guide will be found at the end of this chapter to use as a model when you work with your buyer.

After filling out the guide privately, your buyer will be better able to determine on his own if he qualifies for a loan. Even if your buyer is on the borderline, encourage him to speak to a bank officer. There are times when extenuating circumstances will allow the bank to make a loan to a seemingly unqualified buyer.

Mortgages

There are three basic types of loans available to the home buyer: the conventional mortgage, the F.H.A.-insured mortgage and the V.A.-guaranteed mortgage.

The conventional mortgage is a loan extended by a lending institution to the buyer to finance a home purchase, without any insurance or government guarantee. Most conventional loans now carry an interest rate ranging from 7 to 9 percent and sometimes higher. Most conventional loans require a down payment of between 25 and 40 percent of the purchase price. The advantage of a conventional loan over an insured loan is that it is easier to obtain and usually allows a lower percentage as a down payment.

An F.H.A.-insured loan insures the lending institution against default on the part of the borrower. (Banks are usually ready to accept these types of mortgages as they offer the least risk to the lender.) The F.H.A. (Federal Housing Administration) is not providing the money, they are just guaranteeing loans made by private institutions. These loans must meet certain standards set by the F.H.A., such as maximum interest rates.

With V.A. (Veterans Administration) loans the money again is provided by private lending institutions. The government insures a portion of the loan, up to 60 percent. Your buyer must be related to the armed services, either as a veteran or as an active participant, to qualify for a V.A.-insured loan. The real advantage here is that the money can be borrowed with a smaller down payment.

With the F.H.A.-insured loan the borrower must pay a premium (for insurance purposes) of 1 percent of the loan amount. The V.A.-insured loan requires no premium, but the borrower is responsible for any loss suffered by the agency in case of default.

There will be a disparity in interest rates between V.A. or F.H.A. loans and conventional home loans. If the maximum rate of interest on an insured loan is 7 percent (by federal law) and the conventional loan interest rate is 8 percent, the lending institution carrying the existing mortgage will make up the difference by charging "points" making up the difference between the interest allowed by law and the interest the lender will collect. *F.H.A. regulations forbid the charging of mortgage points to the buyer so the seller, if he wants to make this sale, will have to pay the additional points himself.* This money is usually deducted from the cash the seller receives after the sale is completed. The seller, who can anticipate this charge, can just raise his asking price sufficiently to cover the difference.

The disadvantage in dealing with a buyer who is obtaining either F.H.A.- or V.A.-guaranteed loans is the enormous amount of paper work involved before the buyer finds out if he is eligible. This may take up to two months, during which time your house may be off the market. If you do not want to lose this valuable selling time, accept your prospect's binder only on the condition that your house is to remain on the market during that period. You will then have the opportunity to meet with other potential buyers while your prime prospect is sweating out his mortgage application.

If your buyer cannot obtain a home loan from any of the major sources of home moneylenders, there are ways you may help him obtain his financing.

Existing Mortgages

If you have an existing mortgage on your house you may be able to arrange for your buyer to assume it. Of course, this requires the approval of the lender. Their concern will be whether your buyer is credit worthy. (If you have an F.H.A.- or V.A.-approved mortgage on your home, you will be able to transfer the mortgage only with the consent of the appropriate agency.)

You may run into a problem getting your lender to exchange the loan in a period of rising interest rates. Banks are not anxious to re-lend money at old, lower interest rates. This is especially true if you got your mortgage years ago when interest rates were at their lowest.

If your bank does allow your buyer to assume your

existing mortgage, there are certain precautions you must take to release yourself from liability. You must obtain the buyer's release from liability so you will not be held responsible for payments if he defaults. The mortgage should be drawn up in the buyer's name and not just endorsed over to him by you. Only in this way are you released from all responsibility for the mortgage.

Second Mortgages

Another alternative is to give your buyer a second mortgage. In this case, you lend your own money to the buyer to help him make his down payment. Consider this type of loan only if your income is strong and the purchase price high enough to warrant investing your money in the transaction.

Of course, there is a higher risk with a second mortgage than with a conventional loan and, therefore, higher interest rates are usually charged (somewhere between 8 and 10 percent). The terms between the buyer and you should be arranged by your attorney.

Be sure your attorney inserts a "due on sale" clause in the second mortgage. In the event the buyer sells the property before the mortgage is paid off he will have to pay the full amount due you on the note before he can complete the sale of his property. And you, of course, want to avoid the risk of the buyer passing his second mortgage on to a third party.

Contracts

If your buyer has the cash for the necessary down payment but does not qualify for a loan, you may consider selling your house on contract. In this case you will take the buyer's payments and use them to pay your own mortgage on the house. The buyer is only given the deed to your property when he has made the last payment on the contract.

Contracts like this usually run from five to seven years and require the buyer to refinance the contract when he has paid enough of the principal to become eligible for a regular home loan. Your security lies with your house and the buyer's down payment. Be aware that there can be enormous economic and legal problems selling a house on contract. You should not consider this option until you have discussed all the various possibilities with your lawyer.

Purchase Money Mortgages

You, as the seller, take this mortgage to cover the difference between what the buyer can pay down on your house and the maximum amount of first-mortgage money he can obtain. For example, if the selling price of your house is $40,000 and the buyer can get a $30,000 mortgage but doesn't have the necessary $10,000 for a down payment, you can give him a purchase money mortgage for part of that amount.

You must be certain that the cash down payment the buyer makes is at least sufficient to cover foreclosing costs if the buyer defaults on his payments. It also usually involves a higher interest rate than a regular home loan because of the risk involved.

With either a second mortgage or a purchase money mortgage you may hire a mortgage company to collect the regular mortgage payments for you. The fee is generally 1 percent of the principal per year.

Renting with An Option to Buy

This is an alternative if you don't need the cash from your house sale right away. Your buyer rents your house with an option to buy it at some later date. Of course, this is a last resort, one you should only consider if: You feel you will not be able to sell your house within the time period you have; you are moving out of state and will not be available to show your house to prospective buyers; or you have closed on your new house, and you are in need of the cash you would receive from the monthly rental payments of your old house.

The prospective buyer will rent your house for a period of one year (the usual length of this kind of option) with an option to buy the house after that time. A portion of the monthly payments will be used toward his down payment, with the selling price agreed upon beforehand.

Assuming cash is not your primary need, there are several advantages to this method of "sale." Your house will not sit empty for an extended period of time (empty houses are targets for vandals). Your buyer may pick up the option at the end of the year and buy your property. You will at least be getting some monthly payment to cover costs of the mortgage and utilities, and money you receive beyond your expenses is profit.

Of course, your house will be off the market for the period of time designated in your tenant's lease. And you will now be a landlord, responsible for major repairs and maintenance.

Take certain precautions if you decide to rent with an option to buy. You should require your tenants to make a security payment to cover any damages to your property. This security deposit will be returned in part or in full at the end of the lease depending on the result of an inspection of your property.

You should have all papers drawn up by your attorney. This agreement should include the prearranged selling price, the length of the lease and the amount of monthly payments necessary to cover your tenant's down payment and other fees your tenant will pay if he decides to purchase the property.

Mortgage Buyer's Form

SELLING PRICE $_____

50% DOWN PAYMENT   _____

LOAN AMOUNT $_____

INTEREST RATE   _____%

TERM   _____YRS.

MONTHLY PRINCIPAL
  & INTEREST $_____

POINTS   _____

Name of lending institution _____
Telephone number _____
Spoke to _____

Mortgage Buyer's Form

SELLING PRICE $_____

25% DOWN PAYMENT   _____

LOAN AMOUNT $_____

INTEREST RATE   _____%

TERM   _____YRS.

MONTHLY PRINCIPAL
    & INTEREST $_____

POINTS   _____

Name of lending institution _____

Telephone number _____

Spoke to _____

MORTGAGE BUYER'S FORM

SELLING PRICE $_____

15% DOWN PAYMENT   _____

LOAN AMOUNT $_____

INTEREST RATE   _____%

TERM   _____YRS.

MONTHLY PRINCIPAL
   & INTEREST $_____

POINTS   _____

Name of lending institution _____
Telephone number _____
Spoke to _____

PURCHASE PRICE $_____

MINUS—DOWN PAYMENT

(_____%)   _____

EQUALS—AMOUNT OF

   LOAN $_____

_____

MONTHLY PRINCIPAL

   & INTEREST $_____

PLUS—MONTHLY

   INSURANCE & TAXES   _____

EQUALS—TOTAL MONTHLY

   PAYMENT   _____

                        X 12

TIMES—12 (MONTHS)   _____

EQUALS—ANNUAL PAYMENT   _____

                        X 4

TIMES—4   _____

EQUALS—REQUIRED GROSS

   ANNUAL SALARY $_____

_____

Loan Amortization Tables

Figures on the following tables have been rounded to whole dollars. For a guarantee of absolute accuracy, to the penny, you are advised to check a mortgage payment book from a bank or other lending institution. The figures here include interest and principal only. In many communities, property taxes are added on to monthly payments by the mortgage lender.

MONTHLY PAYMENT
NECESSARY TO AMORTIZE A LOAN—6%

$ Amount	15 yrs.	20 yrs.	25 yrs.	30 yrs.	35 yrs.
15,000	127	107	97	90	86
16,000	135	115	103	96	91
17,000	143	122	110	102	97
18,000	152	129	116	108	103
19,000	160	136	122	114	108
20,000	169	143	129	120	114
21,000	177	150	135	126	120
22,000	186	158	142	132	125
23,000	194	165	148	138	131
24,000	203	172	155	144	137
25,000	211	179	161	150	143
26,000	219	186	168	156	148
27,000	228	193	174	162	154
28,000	236	201	180	168	160
29,000	245	208	187	174	165
30,000	253	215	193	180	171
31,000	262	222	200	186	177
32,000	270	229	206	192	182
33,000	278	236	213	198	188
34,000	287	244	219	204	194
35,000	295	251	226	210	200
36,000	304	258	232	216	205
37,000	312	265	238	222	211
38,000	321	272	245	228	217
39,000	329	279	251	234	222
40,000	338	287	258	240	228
41,000	346	294	264	246	234
42,000	359	301	271	252	239
43,000	363	308	277	258	245
44,000	371	315	284	264	251
45,000	380	322	290	270	257
50,000	421	358	322	300	285
55,000	464	394	354	330	314

$ Amount	15 yrs.	20 yrs.	25 yrs.	30 yrs.	35 yrs.
15,000	129	110	99	92	88
16,000	137	117	106	99	94
17,000	146	124	112	105	100
18,000	154	132	119	111	106
19,000	163	139	125	117	112
20,000	171	146	132	123	117
21,000	180	154	139	130	123
22,000	189	161	145	135	129
23,000	197	168	152	142	135
24,000	206	175	158	148	141
25,000	214	183	165	154	147
26,000	223	190	172	160	153
27,000	232	197	178	166	159
28,000	240	205	185	172	164
29,000	249	212	191	179	170
30,000	257	219	198	185	176
31,000	266	227	205	191	182
32,000	274	234	211	197	188
33,000	283	241	218	203	194
34,000	292	249	224	209	200
35,000	300	256	231	216	205
36,000	309	263	237	222	211
37,000	317	270	244	228	217
38,000	326	278	251	234	223
39,000	334	285	257	240	229
40,000	343	292	264	246	235
41,000	352	300	270	252	241
42,000	360	307	277	259	247
43,000	369	314	284	265	252
44,000	377	322	290	271	258
45,000	386	329	297	277	264
50,000	429	365	330	308	294
55,000	472	402	363	339	323

MONTHLY PAYMENT
NECESSARY TO AMORTIZE A LOAN—6½%

$ Amount	15 yrs.	20 yrs.	25 yrs.	30 yrs.	35 yrs.
15,000	131	112	101	95	88
16,000	139	119	108	101	97
17,000	148	127	115	107	103
18,000	157	134	122	114	109
19,000	166	142	128	120	115
20,000	174	149	135	126	121
21,000	183	157	142	133	127
22,000	192	164	149	139	133
23,000	200	171	155	145	139
24,000	209	179	162	152	145
25,000	218	186	169	158	151
26,000	226	194	176	164	157
27,000	235	201	182	171	163
28,000	244	209	189	177	169
29,000	253	216	196	183	175
30,000	261	224	203	190	181
31,000	270	231	209	196	187
32,000	279	239	216	202	193
33,000	287	246	223	209	199
34,000	296	254	230	215	205
35,000	305	261	236	221	211
36,000	314	268	243	228	218
37,000	322	276	250	234	224
38,000	331	283	257	240	230
39,000	340	291	263	247	236
40,000	348	298	270	253	242
41,000	357	306	277	259	248
42,000	366	313	284	265	254
43,000	375	321	290	272	260
44,000	383	328	297	278	266
45,000	392	336	304	284	272
50,000	436	373	338	316	302
55,000	479	410	371	348	332

$ Amount	15 yrs.	20 yrs.	25 yrs.	30 yrs.	35 yrs.
15,000	133	114	104	97	93
16,000	142	122	111	104	99
17,000	150	129	117	110	106
18,000	159	137	124	117	112
19,000	168	144	131	123	118
20,000	177	152	138	130	124
21,000	186	160	145	136	131
22,000	195	167	152	143	137
23,000	204	175	159	149	143
24,000	212	182	166	156	149
25,000	221	190	173	162	155
26,000	230	198	180	169	162
27,000	239	205	187	175	168
28,000	248	213	193	182	174
29,000	257	221	200	188	180
30,000	265	228	207	195	186
31,000	274	236	214	201	193
32,000	283	243	221	208	199
33,000	292	251	228	214	205
34,000	301	259	235	221	211
35,000	310	266	242	227	218
36,000	319	274	249	234	224
37,000	327	281	256	240	230
38,000	336	289	263	246	236
39,000	345	297	269	253	242
40,000	354	304	276	259	249
41,000	363	312	283	266	255
42,000	372	319	290	272	261
43,000	381	327	297	279	267
44,000	389	335	304	285	273
45,000	398	342	311	292	280
50,000	442	380	345	324	311
55,000	487	418	380	357	342

MONTHLY PAYMENT
NECESSARY TO AMORTIZE A LOAN—7%

$ Amount	15 yrs.	20 yrs.	25 yrs.	30 yrs.	35 yrs.
15,000	135	116	106	100	96
16,000	144	124	113	106	102
17,000	153	132	120	113	109
18,000	162	140	127	120	115
19,000	171	147	134	126	121
20,000	180	155	141	133	128
21,000	189	163	148	140	134
22,000	198	171	156	146	141
23,000	207	178	163	153	147
24,000	216	186	169	160	153
25,000	225	194	177	166	160
26,000	234	202	184	173	166
27,000	243	209	191	180	173
28,000	252	217	198	186	179
29,000	261	225	205	193	185
30,000	270	233	212	200	192
31,000	279	240	219	206	198
32,000	288	248	226	213	204
33,000	297	256	233	220	211
34,000	306	264	240	226	217
35,000	315	271	247	233	224
36,000	324	279	254	240	230
37,000	333	287	262	246	236
38,000	342	295	269	253	243
39,000	351	302	276	259	249
40,000	359	310	283	266	256
41,000	369	318	290	273	262
42,000	378	326	297	279	268
43,000	387	333	304	286	275
44,000	395	341	311	293	281
45,000	404	349	318	299	287
50,000	449	388	353	333	319
55,000	494	426	389	366	351

MONTHLY PAYMENT
NECESSARY TO AMORTIZE A LOAN—7¼%

$ Amount	15 yrs.	20 yrs.	25 yrs.	30 yrs.	35 yrs.
15,000	137	119	108	102	98
16,000	146	126	116	109	105
17,000	155	134	123	116	112
18,000	164	142	130	121	118
19,000	173	150	137	130	125
20,000	183	158	145	136	131
21,000	192	166	152	143	138
22,000	201	174	159	150	144
23,000	210	182	166	157	151
24,000	219	190	173	164	158
25,000	228	198	181	171	164
26,000	237	206	188	177	171
27,000	246	213	195	184	177
28,000	256	221	202	191	184
29,000	266	229	210	198	190
30,000	274	237	217	205	197
31,000	283	245	224	211	204
32,000	292	253	231	218	210
33,000	301	261	239	225	217
34,000	310	269	246	232	223
35,000	320	277	253	239	230
36,000	329	285	260	246	236
37,000	338	292	267	252	243
38,000	347	300	275	259	249
39,000	356	308	282	266	256
40,000	365	316	289	273	263
41,000	374	324	296	280	269
42,000	383	332	304	287	276
43,000	393	340	311	293	282
44,000	402	348	318	300	289
45,000	411	356	325	307	295
50,000	456	395	361	341	328
55,000	502	435	398	375	361

MONTHLY PAYMENT
NECESSARY TO AMORTIZE A LOAN—7½%

$ Amount	15 yrs.	20 yrs.	25 yrs.	30 yrs.	35 yrs.
15,000	139	121	111	105	101
16,000	148	129	118	112	108
17,000	158	137	126	119	115
18,000	167	145	133	125	121
19,000	176	153	140	133	128
20,000	185	161	148	140	135
21,000	195	169	155	147	142
22,000	204	177	163	154	148
23,000	213	185	170	161	155
24,000	222	193	177	168	162
25,000	232	201	185	175	169
26,000	241	209	192	182	175
27,000	250	218	200	189	182
28,000	260	226	207	196	189
29,000	269	234	214	203	196
30,000	278	242	222	210	202
31,000	287	250	229	217	209
32,000	297	258	236	224	216
33,000	306	266	244	231	223
34,000	315	274	251	238	229
35,000	324	282	259	245	236
36,000	334	290	266	252	243
37,000	343	298	273	259	249
38,000	352	306	281	266	256
39,000	362	314	288	273	263
40,000	371	322	296	280	270
41,000	380	330	302	287	276
42,000	389	338	310	294	283
43,000	399	346	318	301	290
44,000	408	354	325	308	297
45,000	417	363	333	315	303
50,000	464	403	370	350	337
55,000	510	443	406	385	371

MONTHLY PAYMENT
NECESSARY TO AMORTIZE A LOAN—7¾%

$ Amount	15 yrs.	20 yrs.	25 yrs.	30 yrs.	35 yrs.
15,000	141	123	113	107	104
16,000	151	131	121	115	111
17,000	160	140	128	122	118
18,000	169	148	136	129	125
19,000	179	156	144	136	132
20,000	188	164	151	143	138
21,000	198	172	159	150	145
22,000	207	181	166	158	152
23,000	217	189	173	165	159
24,000	226	197	181	172	166
25,000	235	205	189	179	173
26,000	245	213	196	186	180
27,000	254	222	204	193	187
28,000	264	230	212	201	194
29,000	273	238	219	208	201
30,000	282	246	227	215	208
31,000	292	255	234	222	215
32,000	301	263	242	229	222
33,000	311	271	249	236	228
34,000	320	279	257	244	235
35,000	329	287	264	251	242
36,000	339	296	272	258	249
37,000	348	304	279	265	256
38,000	358	312	287	272	263
39,000	367	320	295	279	270
40,000	377	328	302	287	277
41,000	386	337	310	294	284
42,000	395	345	317	301	291
43,000	405	353	325	308	298
44,000	414	361	332	315	305
45,000	424	369	340	322	311
50,000	471	410	378	358	346
55,000	518	452	415	394	381

MONTHLY PAYMENT
NECESSARY TO AMORTIZE A LOAN—8%

$ Amount	15 yrs.	20 yrs.	25 yrs.	30 yrs.	35 yrs.
15,000	143	125	116	110	107
16,000	153	134	124	117	114
17,000	162	142	131	125	121
18,000	172	151	139	132	128
19,000	182	159	147	139	135
20,000	191	167	154	147	142
21,000	201	176	162	154	149
22,000	210	184	170	161	156
23,000	220	192	178	169	163
24,000	229	201	185	176	170
25,000	239	209	193	183	178
26,000	248	217	201	191	185
27,000	258	226	208	198	192
28,000	268	234	216	205	199
29,000	277	243	224	213	206
30,000	287	251	232	220	213
31,000	296	259	239	227	220
32,000	306	268	247	235	227
33,000	315	276	255	242	234
34,000	325	284	262	249	241
35,000	334	293	270	257	249
36,000	344	301	278	264	256
37,000	354	309	286	272	263
38,000	363	318	293	279	270
39,000	373	326	301	286	277
40,000	382	335	309	294	284
41,000	392	343	316	301	291
42,000	401	351	324	308	298
43,000	411	360	332	316	305
44,000	420	368	340	323	313
45,000	430	376	347	330	320
50,000	478	418	386	367	355
55,000	526	460	425	404	391

MONTHLY PAYMENT
NECESSARY TO AMORTIZE A LOAN—8¼%

$ Amount	15 yrs.	20 yrs.	25 yrs.	30 yrs.	35 yrs.
15,000	146	128	118	113	109
16,000	155	136	126	120	117
17,000	165	145	134	128	124
18,000	175	153	142	135	131
19,000	184	162	150	143	138
20,000	194	170	158	150	146
21,000	204	179	166	158	153
22,000	213	187	173	165	160
23,000	223	196	181	173	168
24,000	234	205	189	180	175
25,000	243	213	197	188	182
26,000	252	222	205	195	189
27,000	262	230	213	203	197
28,000	272	239	221	210	204
29,000	281	247	229	218	211
30,000	291	256	237	225	219
31,000	301	264	244	233	226
32,000	310	273	252	240	233
33,000	320	281	260	248	240
34,000	330	290	268	255	248
35,000	340	298	276	263	255
36,000	349	307	284	270	262
37,000	359	315	292	278	270
38,000	369	324	300	285	277
39,000	378	332	308	293	284
40,000	388	341	315	301	291
41,000	398	349	323	308	299
42,000	407	358	331	316	306
43,000	417	366	339	323	313
44,000	427	375	347	331	321
45,000	437	383	355	338	328
50,000	485	426	394	376	364
55,000	534	469	434	413	401

MONTHLY PAYMENT
NECESSARY TO AMORTIZE A LOAN—8½%

$ Amount	15 yrs.	20 yrs.	25 yrs.	30 yrs.	35 yrs.
15,000	148	130	121	115	112
16,000	158	139	129	123	120
17,000	167	148	137	131	127
18,000	177	156	145	138	134
19,000	187	165	153	146	142
20,000	197	174	161	154	149
21,000	207	182	169	161	157
22,000	217	191	177	169	164
23,000	227	200	185	177	172
24,000	236	208	193	185	179
25,000	246	217	201	192	187
26,000	256	226	209	200	194
27,000	266	234	217	208	202
28,000	276	243	225	215	209
29,000	286	252	234	223	217
30,000	295	260	242	231	224
31,000	305	269	250	238	232
32,000	315	278	258	246	239
33,000	325	286	266	254	246
34,000	335	295	274	261	254
35,000	345	304	282	269	261
36,000	355	312	290	277	269
37,000	364	321	298	285	276
38,000	374	330	306	292	284
39,000	384	338	314	300	291
40,000	394	347	322	308	299
41,000	404	356	330	315	306
42,000	414	365	338	323	314
43,000	423	373	346	331	321
44,000	433	382	354	338	329
45,000	443	391	362	346	336
50,000	492	434	403	384	373
55,000	542	477	443	423	411

MONTHLY PAYMENT
NECESSARY TO AMORTIZE A LOAN—8¾%

$ Amount	15 yrs.	20 yrs.	25 yrs.	30 yrs.	35 yrs.
15,000	150	133	123	118	115
16,000	160	141	132	126	122
17,000	170	150	140	134	130
18,000	180	159	148	142	138
19,000	190	168	156	150	145
20,000	200	177	164	157	153
21,000	210	186	173	165	161
22,000	220	194	181	173	168
23,000	230	203	189	181	176
24,000	240	212	197	189	184
25,000	250	221	206	197	191
26,000	260	230	214	205	199
27,000	270	239	222	212	207
28,000	280	247	230	220	214
29,000	290	256	238	228	222
30,000	300	265	247	236	230
31,000	310	274	255	244	237
32,000	320	283	263	252	245
33,000	330	292	271	260	253
34,000	340	300	280	267	260
35,000	350	309	288	275	268
36,000	360	318	296	283	276
37,000	370	327	304	291	283
38,000	380	336	312	299	291
39,000	390	345	321	307	299
40,000	400	353	329	315	306
41,000	410	362	337	323	314
42,000	420	371	345	330	321
43,000	430	380	354	338	329
44,000	440	389	362	346	337
45,000	450	398	370	354	344
50,000	500	442	411	393	383
55,000	550	486	452	433	421

MONTHLY PAYMENT
NECESSARY TO AMORTIZE A LOAN—9%

$ Amount	15 yrs.	20 yrs.	25 yrs.	30 yrs.	35 yrs.
15,000	152	135	126	121	118
16,000	162	144	134	129	125
17,000	172	153	143	137	133
18,000	183	162	151	145	141
19,000	193	171	159	153	149
20,000	203	180	168	161	157
21,000	213	189	176	169	164
22,000	223	198	185	177	173
23,000	233	207	193	185	180
24,000	243	216	201	193	188
25,000	254	225	210	201	196
26,000	264	234	218	209	204
27,000	274	243	227	217	212
28,000	284	252	235	225	220
29,000	294	261	243	233	227
30,000	304	270	252	241	235
31,000	314	279	260	249	243
32,000	325	288	269	257	251
33,000	335	297	277	266	259
34,000	345	306	285	274	267
35,000	355	315	294	282	274
36,000	365	324	302	290	282
37,000	375	333	311	298	290
38,000	385	342	319	306	298
39,000	396	351	327	314	306
40,000	406	360	336	322	314
41,000	416	369	344	330	321
42,000	426	378	352	338	329
43,000	436	387	361	346	337
44,000	446	396	369	354	345
45,000	456	405	378	362	353
50,000	507	450	420	402	392
55,000	558	495	462	443	431

133

CHAPTER
6

How to Use This Book if You Are Buying a House

If you're planning to buy a house—and most home sellers are also home buyers—many of the hints and shortcuts that were useful to the seller can be turned around and used to your advantage as a buyer.

The seller's most important task is to get his house in shape to make the fastest, most profitable sale. You, now as the buyer, have two important jobs. One, to determine how much you are willing—and able—to *spend* for a house and, two, to buy a house to your tastes at the lowest possible price.

How much can you afford to pay? The simplest way to get a bead on your financial capabilities is to prepare a budget chart. The following guide may be helpful.

Gross monthly income
of husband & wife $_____

Subtract the total of the
following monthly
expenses from your
monthly income:

FOOD	$_____
CLOTHING	_____
INSTALLMENT DEBTS	_____
AUTOMOBILE PAYMENTS	_____
MEDICAL EXPENSES	_____
LIFE INSURANCE	_____
TUITION OR OTHER EDUCATION EXPENSES	_____
TAXES (FEDERAL, STATE OR CITY, SOCIAL SECURITY, ETC.)	_____
ENTERTAINMENT (INCLUDING GIFTS)	_____
COMMUTING	_____
OTHER FIXED EXPENSES	_____
REGULAR SAVINGS	_____ $_____

$_____

With the use of the mortgage qualification chart at
the end of Chapter 5 you will be able to determine
how much you can afford to pay for a house.

Here are some general rules of thumb to give you an

additional way to estimate your budget: Do not spend more than 25 percent of your yearly income to pay for a house and, monthly mortgage expenses should total 1 percent or less of the purchase price. If your budget fits these two categories you can assume that you will be a good candidate for a mortgage loan.

Begin your search for a new house by ruling out all classified ads for houses that are way out of your price range. It's depressing to see extravagant homes that you might certainly like but cannot afford. And you're wasting your time visiting homes that are very much lower in price. Do see all those houses selling for a few thousand dollars more or less than you want to spend. This will give you a good general idea of the house market in that community.

There will be some houses that cost more than you want to spend, but the owners have given signals like "willing to negotiate," "financing available," or "have to leave." These houses may actually sell for considerably less than their advertised asking price, and you should take the time to see them.

Get in touch with as many people as you know who live in the area you're interested in and check how much houses are selling for, or have sold for, in their neighborhood. Ask your acquaintances to recommend any houses that might appeal to you. In addition to the newspapers, check local bulletin boards and community groups for listings.

If someone in the family will be working for a large company in the area call the company's placement office, they usually keep records of houses available for sale in the vicinity. If you are a student or faculty member be sure to contact the local university housing office for lists of homes for sale.

The Neighborhood

Spend a few weekend afternoons driving through neighborhoods that appeal to you. Not only will you get a better feel for certain communities, but you can check for "For Sale" signs.

Take advantage of open houses, even if the house is above the price range you had in mind. These visits will give you an indication of the type of people that live in that particular neighborhood and will help you determine whether you will be happy in that area of town. You can also pick up decorating hints by visiting these homes.

Let's say that you've driven through the neighborhood a number of times, have called a few prospective sellers, and visited a number of open houses. Of all the houses you have seen there are maybe two or three worth considering. Let's take a tour of one hypothetical house and discuss what features should be looked at very carefully.

You can make reasonably sound judgments about houses even if you're not an architect or professional appraiser. You'll be helped by an understanding of good construction techniques, but even more important is to know when it's imperative to seek outside help.

Begin by checking the surrounding houses. Is the neighborhood well kept? Are the lawns well tended? Is the house you're interested in the only one around that has a fresh paint job or a beautifully kept garden? You must keep in mind that the surrounding area will be a vital factor when you try to resell. If the neighborhood is sliding down, your house, even if it's well kept, will not go up in value no matter how well you keep it.

Avoid buying a house for $50,000 in a neighborhood

of $30,000 homes. You'll have a tough time recovering your investment when it comes time to sell. Also avoid houses that cost and look like much less than the surrounding homes. It will suffer by comparison and will not increase in value as much as neighboring homes. The only exception to this rule are the so-called "fixer-uppers." These are the homes, in better neighborhoods, that can benefit enormously from structural and decorating improvements. If you have the money to redesign and renovate the house to conform to neighborhood standards then you can consider the investment sound. These homes are usually sold at bargain prices, and if you have the time, money and energy, you could come out far ahead.

The Exterior

Stand in the street in front of the house. Is the lawn well kept? Are bushes dying or in need of pruning? Does the general condition show careless planning? Have the owners tried some cosmetic touches that will fade in six months? Will you have to spend good money to repair cosmetic failures? Check the driveway. Will it need resurfacing soon or maybe even redirection? Can you drive your car to a convenient entrance to the house? Do you have to walk across the lawn to get to the door?

Now take a good look at the outside of the house. Does it need a paint job? Are the sides and back of the exterior of the house in as good shape as the front? Be sure the paint is not flaking or chipped and that the shiny new paint job (if there is one) is more than one layer deep.

Be wary of the picture window that faces your neighbor's picture window? Although attractive in itself, this view means absolutely no privacy.

If the house is a mishmash of design features, no matter how well they are hidden, it is bound to decline in value. Be certain all windows are of the same general shape and design. The house should have a "total look," and not be a thrown-together combination. With new additions in particular, homeowners may go off to a completely different style. The result detracts from the appearance of the house (and from it's value). Any new addition should conform to the form of the original structure, and not look as though it were thrown on as an afterthought.

In terms of space, it's good to keep in mind that a ranch house takes up twice as much space on its lot as a two story house with the same number and size of rooms. Unless the lot is oversized you will be giving up outdoor space for the convenience of one-story living.

One of the most important, less apparent factors to consider in choosing your house is the condition of the roof. The average price of a new roof is $500 to $1,000 —a hefty sum of money to spend after you've moved in. If the roof is in bad condition you must use your judgment in deciding whether you will spend another $1,000 to have it repaired. It's much better to discover the defect in advance and deduct the cost of a new roof from the purchase price of the house.

It's a good idea to carry a notebook with you when you inspect homes. Note all the expenses you are likely to incur if you purchase that house. You can bring these items to the seller's attention when you begin negotiating a selling price.

Is the entrance to the house impressive? Does it give

the appearance of being well-kept? Don't concern yourself with the small details that can easily be repaired.
The bulb that is burned out above the entrance is not a
problem.

The Entrance Hall

The entrance hall or foyer should be inviting. Is there
a closet for guests to hang their coats? Is the space
cramped? Do you have to close the front door to allow
people to enter? Although not the most important
room in the house (many houses don't have any entrance hall) if the space is well-designed it can add
dramatic impact to the house.

The Living Room

The living room is next. Begin your inspection at the
top and work down. Are the ceilings well-plastered? Are
there signs of leakage? Is the wallpaper faded or
stained? It's not likely that you will find a house that is
in perfect condition (unless you are looking at a brand
new house), so you will have to determine whether the
faults can be fixed with little investment of time and
money or whether you will be in for extensive or expensive renovation.

The main thing to note when checking walls and ceilings is whether they will simply require repainting or
will water damage and roofing problems cost thousands
to repair.

The placement of windows, although seemingly not
important, should be given consideration. If the large

picture window fills up the only large wall, your furniture may be difficult to place. Think about the larger pieces of furniture you have and visually place them in the room. Will there be room for your large breakfront? Does your stereo require new shelving? Is there adequate storage space, or built-ins? Is the carpeting in good condition—and is it being left by the owner? Does the carpet color harmonize with your furniture or will you have to remove it anyway?

If pictures seem hung in strange spots around the room, they may be hiding a defect. Don't be embarrassed to look behind them.

Check the view. If you look out onto the garage or some other unsightly feature you may have to cover the windows, and lose the advantage of that light source. Is the owner leaving his drapes or has he offered to sell them to you? Will your own curtains fit these windows or will you have to purchase new ones? Is there a fireplace? Does it function well?

Look at the general character of the rooms. Do they have a typically early American feel, even though your furniture is modern? Is the space adequate for entertaining? Will you have to walk around your large pieces of furniture to get into the room? Do you have to walk through the living room to get to the other parts of the house? Is the living room convenient to the kitchen and the dining room? Does the traffic pattern of the house flow smoothly? Your general feeling about a room, your *first* impression, is a good indication of whether you will be happy with it.

Will the family room or study serve *your* family's needs? If your present home has a den and this house does not, you may find it difficult to adjust to the lack of that room, even if the other rooms are larger.

The Kitchen

The kitchen is the most important room to consider. Not only is it the room in which your family spends a great deal of time, but it is also the room that requires the biggest investment to renovate. If you are used to a large airy kitchen and you spend a great deal of time cooking, a small dark kitchen may not be adequate. If your family is large, small stoves, sinks and refrigerators, no matter how new, will be inadequate.

Space is most important in the kitchen. Is there room for a table and chairs to accommodate your family at mealtimes? Will you have to spend extra time walking from appliance to appliance because of poor placement? If the appliances are adequate in size, are they also in decent condition? New appliances are expensive, and unless you are bringing yours with you, you will be investing hundreds of dollars to buy new ones. If you do plan to bring your appliances with you, measure to be sure they will fit in the spaces allocated.

Turn the water on in the sink. Does it come out instantly? Does the hot water feel hot enough? Is the faucet leaking?

Is there a dishwasher? If you are used to the convenience of one you will find it most inconvenient to be without one.

Is there adequate counter space? Does the owner seem to be crowding everything in one spot because the space is inadequate? Are there pantry facilities? A broom closet? Will you have enough storage space for your own things?

Are the cabinets in need of repainting or refinishing? Consider how much work you will have to invest to make them more attractive. If a new coat of paint is all it will take to make the kitchen more attractive, don't disqualify the house.

The kitchen floor will be a problem if it must be re-covered. Depending on the size of the room, a new kitchen floor could cost $300 to $400, even with inexpensive linoleum.

Does the kitchen have adequate ventilation? If the stove does not have an exhaust fan, and the kitchen is not large and airy, cooking odors will be trapped. Be sure that windows can be opened easily to let cooking odors out, and that there are enough windows to allow for good circulation.

A word about decorating. It is unlikely that your taste will match that of the residents in all the homes you visit. Do not disqualify a house because you don't like the color of the room or the style of curtains. These decorating touches are easily changed. Just be sure that the structural qualities meet with your approval. Work to maintain an open mind. Try to see through the taste differences you may have with the owner.

The Bathrooms

The *number* of bathrooms should be your first concern, especially if you have a large family. If a house appeals to you in every other way but has only one bathroom, expect to spend in the neighborhood of $2,000 to install a new bath.

Now to the condition of the bathrooms. Are the fixtures worn and old-fashioned? Are they badly chipped or discolored? Are there tiles missing from the walls? Is the lighting a problem? If the bathroom is of adequate size but needs renovation, it will probably cost $500 or more to install new fixtures.

Run the water in the sink and the bathtub at the same time, then flush the toilet. Is the pressure adequate? Does the water get hot without having to wait for minutes? Remember an unattractive bathroom could be made more attractive with a coat of paint, but unattractive fixtures require an outlay of hundreds of dollars.

Be sure there are adequate storage facilities in the bathroom. Is there a linen closet with enough space to store supplies? Is there easy access from the bathrooms to the bedrooms? Is there a bathroom for guests?

The Bedrooms

Are there enough bedrooms to satisfy your family's needs? If you are used to having a bedroom for each of your children, will it be difficult to get used to less space?

Are the closets adequate? Are the ceilings peeling and cracked? Will the floors need to be re-covered? Will there be enough space for your bedroom pieces? Will your king-size bed fit into this master bedroom?

The Basement

Spend some time inspecting the basement. It's not the most attractive room in most homes, but it's the mechanical center of the house. Is the furnace clean and new? Check the walls and floor for water seepage. (It's important and should be a major factor in your decision to buy this particular house.)

A natural-gas fueled furnace is cleaner to operate

than an oil furnace. It also costs less to install, less to service, and lasts longer. If the gas is bottled, the fuel costs will go up.

Remember that electric heat is the most expensive to operate. Check with the owner about his heating costs. Ask to see several recent bills.

The hot water heater should have a capacity of 50 gallons for a family of five (this includes the use of a dishwasher and a washing machine). Hot water lines should be insulated to save fuel and to insure instant hot water when you turn on faucets.

Check the wiring (especially in an older house) to see if it is adequate to accommodate appliances you will be bringing with you.

Be sure there are no signs of seepage around the floor where it meets the wall. Check if a new plastering job may have been used to cover up a recent water problem.

Check to make sure the clothes drier has proper outside ventilation and notice whether a dehumidifier has been used in the basement (a possible sign of a moisture problem).

Of course if there are puddles of water on the floor or water stains, the existence of a water problem is obvious. There are a number of ways these problems can be remedied, but it can be expensive. Make sure you know how much it will cost for big repairs before you buy.

If you intend to use the basement as a storage area, moisture will present extra problems. And, wetness will make remodeling the basement almost useless.

If the laundry area is in the basement be sure there is adequate lighting and that the basement dirt won't ruin clean, wet clothes.

Inspect the water supply source. Do you get enough

pressure and supply of water from either a city system or a well for your needs? Is the septic tank or cesspool adequate, and has it been cleaned recently? Will you be able to convert to city sewer lines if they are not already being used?

Inspect the foundation. Is it solid? Are the joints mortared? Look at the foundation from the outside. If there are cracks, it's a sure sign that you'll be in for water leekage.

The Garage

First, see if your car (or cars) fits in the garage, especially in older homes where garages were built for smaller cars. If there is a work area in the garage is there proper ventilation? Are the garage doors working properly? If you intend to use the garage as a storage area, is the space adequate for your needs?

Use the checklists at the end of Chapter 1 as a guide. If the seller does not give you a listing sheet to take home, keep records in your notebook. Write down the name and address of the owner, the number of rooms in the house, special features, items that will be included in the sale of the house, etc. Also make notes of your evaluation of each aspect of the house. When you look at many homes, impressions have a way of evaporating unless you keep records.

You're coming to the home stretch. You've ruled out those houses that don't fit your requirements at all, and settled on one or two that you'd really like to consider seriously. You know the asking price, what it includes, and what it doesn't include.

Negotiation

You have an idea how much the house is worth and how much you can afford to pay. If these two figures are within a couple of thousand dollars of each other, it's time to get down to serious bargaining.

The main point to remember is that the asking price rarely ends up being the selling price.

Your first offer should be less than the figure you could agree to buy the house for. Ask yourself: How realistic is the asking price? How much money will I have to spend to put the house into shape for my family?

If you think the house is overpriced or you anticipate spending "fix-up" money, make your offer accordingly. But, if the house looks in good shape and the asking price seems reasonable, and you still insist on holding out for a lower price, you risk losing the house.

If there seems to be a lot of competition for the house, don't panic. Keep your head. Be reasonable and, if you can afford it, flexible. If you've shopped enough homes, you should have a good idea of the relative value of this house. Just try to avoid the feeling of "I must have this house." If your final price is not acceptable, go on to another house.

If you are firmly committed to buying this house and your offer is accepted, give the seller a deposit and request that he take the house off the market until you get mortgage approval.

As a buyer you will, of course, be trying to use all the techniques at your disposal to get a better deal than the seller wants to give you. The greatest part of this book has been devoted to ways you can sell your house for more than it may be "worth." Basically that means that as a seller you'd be preparing your house to look as sturdy and attractive as possible. If you have learned to put these methods to use as a seller, you now know how to look at a house as a buyer, an educated buyer who can see through attempts to cover a home's faults.